THE DISABLED

Other Books in the Current Controversies Series:

THE DISABLED

David Bender, *Publisher*
Bruno Leone, *Executive Editor*

Scott Barbour, *Managing Editor*
Brenda Stalcup, *Senior Editor*

Brenda Stalcup, *Book Editor*

CURRENT CONTROVERSIES

Cover Photo: © Uniphoto

Library of Congress Cataloging-in-Publication Data

The disabled / Brenda Stalcup, book editor.
        p. cm. — (Current controversies)
     Includes bibliographical references and index.
     ISBN 1-56510-530-3 (lib. bdg. : alk. paper). — ISBN 1-56510-529-X
(pbk. : alk. paper)
     1. Handicapped—Government policy—United States. 2. United
States. Americans with Disabilities Act of 1990. 3. Discrimination
against the handicapped—Law and legislation—United States.
I. Stalcup, Brenda. II. Series.
HV1553.D549   1997
362.4'0973—dc20   96-36099
                                                                CIP

© 1997 by Greenhaven Press, Inc., PO Box 289009, San Diego, CA 92198-9009
Printed in the U.S.A.

Contents

Chapter 3: Should Disabled Children Be Mainstreamed?

Yes: Disabled Children Should Be Mainstreamed

No: Disabled Children Should Not Be Mainstreamed

Chapter 4: What Medical Responses to Disability Are Acceptable?

die is perfectly rational. If a person is too disabled to commit suicide
alone, he or she has the right to request assisted suicide.

Many people believe that the disabled—especially those who have
severe disabilities—have a right to assisted suicide. This belief is
often based on misguided notions about and prejudice against people
with disabilities. If a disabled person is suicidal and depressed, he or
she should be given counseling as well as the assistance necessary to
lead a full and independent life.

Foreword

By definition, controversies are "discussions of questions in which opposing opinions clash" (Webster's Twentieth Century Dictionary Unabridged). Few would deny that controversies are a pervasive part of the human condition and exist on virtually every level of human enterprise. Controversies transpire between individuals and among groups, within nations and between nations. Controversies supply the grist necessary for progress by providing challenges and challengers to the status quo. They also create atmospheres where strife and warfare can flourish. A world without controversies would be a peaceful world; but it also would be, by and large, static and prosaic.

The Series' Purpose

The purpose of the Current Controversies series is to explore many of the social, political, and economic controversies dominating the national and international scenes today. Titles selected for inclusion in the series are highly focused and specific. For example, from the larger category of criminal justice, Current Controversies deals with specific topics such as police brutality, gun control, white collar crime, and others. The debates in Current Controversies also are presented in a useful, timeless fashion. Articles and book excerpts included in each title are selected if they contribute valuable, long-range ideas to the overall debate. And wherever possible, current information is enhanced with historical documents and other relevant materials. Thus, while individual titles are current in focus, every effort is made to ensure that they will not become quickly outdated. Books in the Current Controversies series will remain important resources for librarians, teachers, and students for many years.

In addition to keeping the titles focused and specific, great care is taken in the editorial format of each book in the series. Book introductions and chapter prefaces are offered to provide background material for readers. Chapters are organized around several key questions that are answered with diverse opinions representing all points on the political spectrum. Materials in each chapter include opinions in which authors clearly disagree as well as alternative opinions in which authors may agree on a broader issue but disagree on the possible solutions. In this way, the content of each volume in Current Controversies mirrors the mosaic of opinions encountered in society. Readers will quickly realize that there are many viable answers to these complex issues. By questioning each author's conclusions, students and casual readers can begin to develop the critical thinking skills so important to evaluating opinionated material.

Current Controversies is also ideal for controlled research. Each anthology in the series is composed of primary sources taken from a wide gamut of informational categories including periodicals, newspapers, books, United States and foreign government documents, and the publications of private and public organizations. Readers will find factual support for reports, debates, and research papers covering all areas of important issues. In addition, an annotated table of contents, an index, a book and periodical bibliography, and a list of organizations to contact are included in each book to expedite further research.

Perhaps more than ever before in history, people are confronted with diverse and contradictory information. During the Persian Gulf War, for example, the public was not only treated to minute-to-minute coverage of the war, it was also inundated with critiques of the coverage and countless analyses of the factors motivating U.S. involvement. Being able to sort through the plethora of opinions accompanying today's major issues, and to draw one's own conclusions, can be a complicated and frustrating struggle. It is the editors' hope that Current Controversies will help readers with this struggle.

Introduction

The term "disability" refers to a wide variety of conditions, including blindness, deafness, mental retardation, and mobility impairments. Some health professionals also consider the term to encompass learning disabilities, mental illnesses such as autism, and chronic or long-term illnesses such as epilepsy, diabetes, cancer, or AIDS. Depending on which disabilities are included, estimates of the number of disabled Americans range from 35 million to 43 million. In his 1993 book *No Pity: People with Disabilities Forging a New Civil Rights Movement*, Joseph P. Shapiro notes that "there are some 30 million African-Americans. So, even at the lowest estimate [of 35 million], disabled people could be considered the nation's largest minority."

People who have disabilities face problems stemming from their physical or mental impairments. Someone with mental retardation, for example, may have difficulty learning how to read or handle money, while individuals with cerebral palsy may need assistance in dressing themselves. However, people with disabilities must also deal with obstacles that are manmade or that arise from discrimination against the disabled. For instance, a person who uses a wheelchair may be unable to navigate the grocery store because the checkout aisles are too narrow or too high. Store clerks may refuse to assist a blind person with finding an item or may regularly overcharge mentally retarded customers. Since the mid-1960s, a growing number of activists have sought to overcome such limitations by enforcing legislation that protects the rights of people with disabilities and by changing negative public attitudes about the disabled.

While few would argue that these goals are misguided, critics do contend that the disability-rights movement sometimes goes too far in its efforts to erase the stigma around disability. One of the most heated debates between researchers and disability-rights activists is whether disabilities should be viewed as medical problems to be corrected or as normal physical variations among humans. This disagreement can be illustrated by the controversy surrounding cochlear implants for the deaf.

A cochlear implant is an electronic device that partially replaces the function of a defective cochlea, the organ in the inner ear that sends signals to the auditory nerve. The device has several components: A tiny chip is surgically implanted in the inner ear and a receiver is placed under the skin behind the ear. Wires lead to an earpiece that contains a microphone and to a digital speech processor—about the size of a cigarette pack—that is worn on the belt. The implant converts sounds into electronic signals that are picked up by the auditory nerve and transmitted to the brain. The approximation of hearing that results varies from person to person. About 20 percent of implant recipients hear well enough to understand most spoken sentences, even over the telephone. Another 20 percent receive little or no benefit at all. The majority of recipients gain some hearing but use the implant primarily as an aid to lip-reading. However, additional research promises to make the surgery more successful. With improvements in the device's design, implant researchers believe, the number of deaf people who receive significant benefits may eventually increase from 20 percent to as high as 75 percent.

Most physicians and some deaf individuals maintain that cochlear implants represent a great advancement in the search for a cure for deafness. According to the father of one child who underwent a successful implant operation, "This is a miracle of biblical proportions, making the deaf hear." However, many members of the deaf community oppose cochlear implantation. Noting that the procedure works best for those who lost their hearing after learning to speak, opponents criticize the Food and Drug Administration's approval of cochlear implantations in children who are born deaf. These children, they argue, are rarely able to understand the unfamiliar and often garbled sounds coming from the implant. In his book *Mask of Benevolence: Disabling the Deaf Community*, psychologist Harlan Lane cites studies of speech perception in which children with implants scored the same as or worse than deaf children who used hearing aids.

Furthermore, critics of cochlear implants object to the very idea that deafness is a problem that needs to be fixed. Roslyn Rosen, dean of continuing education at Gallaudet University in Washington, D.C., maintains that "most people view deafness as a pathological condition and as a problem in search of a cure. We don't see ourselves that way. We view ourselves as people who happen to not hear, and for whom life is still very good." Members of the deaf community point out that American Sign Language, not English, is the language they use most fluently and naturally. Along with their separate language, deaf individuals assert, they also have distinct customs and a unique culture. Many argue that the primary obstacle deaf people face is not their inability to hear but rather communication difficulties that typically arise between any two cultures that use different languages. "We consider ourselves more of a cultural group than a medical anomaly," states Nancy Bloch, the executive director of the National Association of the Deaf. Bloch, Rosen, and others criticize the attitude that an invasive and unreliable surgery is better for deaf children than the rich cultural and linguistic heritage of the deaf. Some deaf activists have even characterized cochlear implants as genocide.

Advocates of cochlear implantation view this attitude with dismay. Although medical researchers and physicians may concede that concerns about the survival of deaf culture are valid, they argue that rejecting a potential cure for deafness is too extreme. Numerous doctors and educators contend that deaf children cannot rely on sign language alone if they are to succeed in an English-speaking world. Writing in *Scientific American*, John Rennie notes that parents of deaf children often choose cochlear implant surgery because they are concerned "that deaf children will be shut out of social contacts and jobs if sign language, rather than English, is their native language." Robert Shannon, director of research at the House Ear Institute in Los Angeles, asserts,

> I don't think that even the most radical members of the deaf community would be able to make a very good case that deaf people are well integrated into society at large. They aren't, and they cannot be, because most of our cultural interactions occur through spoken language.

Deaf children who undergo the cochlear implant surgery at an early age will stand a better chance of learning English and coping with the speaking world, Shannon and others maintain. "If there's a way we can overcome the hearing problems that these people have," Shannon asks, "why should we ignore it?"

Some people who are deaf or who have other disabilities are also wary about the contention that deafness is not a medical problem and should not be corrected. While these individuals may take pride in their abilities and in the deaf culture, they also welcome the possibility of regaining part or all of their hearing. "I would never want to move away from my Deaf identity," states deaf actress and American Sign Language translator Jackie Roth. "But if I could have full hearing, without complications, I would like to have it." In fact, reports Andrew Solomon, a contributing writer for the *New York Times Magazine*, many deaf people disagree with the opponents of cochlear implantation and are "righteously indignant at the thought of a politically correct group suggesting that their problems [are]n't problems." Others who have already undergone the cochlear implant procedure maintain that the benefits outweigh any costs. As Joanne Syrja, who had a cochlear implant performed at the age of 44, explains it,

> I spoke to a person who is mobility impaired, and I said, "What do you think about all this stuff that the spokespeople for the deaf community are saying about how you're better off just being deaf?" After all, there are many things I learned being deaf. He said to me, "Yeah, I learned a lot of stuff, too, from my handicap, but you know what? If I could walk again, I'd throw it all in a hole."

The cochlear implant controversy involves not only questions about the effectiveness of the procedure but also the larger issue of how people with disabilities should be viewed. Many disability-rights advocates contend that the disabled are a minority group that suffers from discrimination. In their opinion, activists should concentrate on promoting acceptance of people with disabilities as valuable members of society. Other commentators argue that science should focus on eliminating disabilities entirely so that in the future no one will face the problems that having a disability can entail. *The Disabled: Current Controversies* examines this debate as well as other social, legal, educational, and ethical issues associated with disability.

Chapter 1

Is the Americans with Disabilities Act (ADA) Effective?

Chapter Preface

The Americans with Disabilities Act (ADA) was signed into law by President George Bush on July 26, 1990. The law prohibited discrimination against the disabled by employers and required that commercial establishments, public accommodations, and mass transportation be made accessible to disabled persons. The various provisions of the ADA went into effect between January 26, 1992, and July 26, 1994.

The ADA was widely touted as the first civil rights protection for people with physical and mental disabilities. Disability-rights activists argue that in the past, the disabled have been held back more by prejudice and lack of access than by their physical limitations. A 1986 poll, for example, found that 66 percent of people with disabilities were unemployed, even though the majority considered themselves able and willing to work. In the same poll, 40 percent said that they frequently encountered physical barriers that barred their access to public places. As Elizabeth Gaspard, who uses a wheelchair, asserts, "Equal employment won't do a thing for me if transit passes me by on the street or I can't get in the front door." According to proponents of the legislation, the ADA ensures that people with disabilities will no longer be excluded from the workplace and from society. Justin Dart, a leader of the disability-rights movement, maintains that "the ADA is working as intended to effect voluntary change in millions of minds, public facilities, and places of employment."

Opponents of the ADA, however, argue that the law places an unreasonable financial burden on employers. Critics cite numerous stories of businessowners who were required to spend thousands of dollars in remodeling costs to accommodate a few disabled customers. Some disability-rights advocates also argue that the ADA has not been effective. According to disabilities policy consultant William T. Bolte, the ADA "makes no distinction between severe disabilities and disabilities that cause inconvenience." The majority of discrimination cases filed under the ADA, he contends, have involved ailments such as carpal tunnel syndrome rather than blindness, multiple sclerosis, or other traditional disabilities. Bolte and others note that unemployment among the seriously disabled has actually increased since the passage of the ADA.

While some commentators praise the ADA, other critics argue that the law either goes too far or does not do enough. Whether this legislation effectively safeguards the rights of disabled Americans is debated in the following chapter.

The ADA Safeguards Civil Rights

by Tony Coelho

About the author: *Tony Coelho, a former U.S. representative, is the chairman of the President's Committee on Employment of People with Disabilities.*

I am a former member of Congress who served for 10 years in the House of Representatives.

During that time and after leaving Congress I worked hard for passage of the Americans With Disabilities Act.

It is the one piece of legislation I am most proud of helping to write because it means so much to so many people, and because it can do so much to make this a better country. . . .

I am one of the 49 million Americans with disabilities. Because of my disability, I have felt the heavy hand of oppression and discrimination.

I didn't like it when it happened to me, and I don't want it happening to anyone else. Never, ever again!

An End to Discrimination

ADA is helping to change things. No more will a blind person be denied entry to a restaurant. No more will someone in a wheelchair be refused entry to a movie theater.

No more will we be turned away from stores, places of entertainment or the workplace because we have a disability. That's important to me.

It's important to the whole country, for a lot of reasons. Not least among them is the growing shortage of skilled labor.

Leaders of the business community have told us they are running out of people and demand will increase for qualified workers at all levels over the next 15 years.

To make up the shortfall, more and more companies are beginning to look at people with disabilities as a resource.

From Tony Coelho, "Freedom for People with Disabilities: Equal Treatment, Equal Opportunity, and an Equal Chance," a speech delivered to the 47th Annual Conference of the President's Committee on Employment of People with Disabilities, Atlanta, Georgia, May 18, 1994.

Businesses are also looking for new markets. So how about 49 million customers!

The disability community has multiple product needs.

Many of you know that and are tapping into this multibillion dollar market that knows from your products, locations, access and attitude whether you are talking to us and want our business.

I believe people with disabilities have a lot to offer America as workers, customers and citizens.

That's why, when the White House asked me how I could best serve the President and his administration, I didn't have to think twice.

I immediately responded that it would be as Chairman of the President's Committee on Employment of People with Disabilities.

> *"People with disabilities have a lot to offer America as workers, customers and citizens."*

I am honored that President Clinton has chosen me to carry forward his agenda in a position that will allow me to continue to fight for independence and equality for people with disabilities.

This is more than a job to me—it is the continuation of a calling that has become my personal ministry.

Correcting the injustices people with disabilities have suffered for so long has become a mission in life for me.

My agenda is to halt discrimination against people with disabilities. *Now.* Not in stages or incrementally, but immediately.

The time has ended for meekly accepting second-class citizenship.

No more will we stand quietly at the end of the line, waiting patiently for the rights that are due us as citizens, voters and taxpayers.

And no more will we allow others to break into line in front of us, or settle for half measures.

We want it all—everything we are entitled to as citizens of the United States. Nothing more—but not one bit less!

A Fair Chance

We want equal treatment, equal opportunity and an equal chance to make it or not on our own merits.

No pity. No preferences. No quotas. No special treatment. Just a fair chance to compete based on our qualifications and ability to contribute.

In other words, my friends, we want nothing less than our freedom.

But freedom has never been won easily. As Gina McDonald, a leader of the Independent Living Movement, has so eloquently stated: "Freedom is rarely given by the oppressor. It must be demanded by the oppressed."

She is absolutely right. As we continue our fight for equality and freedom, let us always remember that empowerment is not a gift to be given, but a right to be claimed.

It is never bestowed from above. It is grasped from below by those with the courage and persistence to make good on their rightful claim.

One other thing. Our demands for equality are not negotiable.

We don't intend to bargain with anybody about our basic civil rights!

This is not the Clean Air Act. What we are talking about is the fundamental precept of citizenship.

As your new chairman, I know you are interested in my priorities and my programs for the President's Committee.

My priorities are identical to yours—those which were expressed by disability leaders in the 60 teleconferences sponsored [in 1993] by the President's Committee.

Those statewide teleconferences were conducted to identify the major issues affecting people with disabilities.

My focus will be on achieving the objectives you have identified, and which we have forwarded in a report to the President and the Congress.

These are clear statements of purpose on which we all agree. We know what we need. Now we need to do it.

My job will be to make sure it gets done. And with your help I will!

Foremost among our objectives are health care reform and ADA implementation.

"ADA . . . is required to assure the fundamental rights of 49 million American citizens."

Health care reform is too complicated for me to deal with in much detail here.

But what we want is not complicated at all. It can be summed up in six simple words: "no exceptions," "no conditions," "no cancellations."

Legislation that meets these basic requirements will be a big step in the right direction.

Implementing the ADA

ADA implementation is our other top priority. Our position on this is even easier to summarize. It is: "no excuses."

Compliance is not optional. ADA is the law of the land, and its observance is required to assure the fundamental rights of 49 million American citizens.

I said "required," not "requested." We won't back down and we won't debate.

One of the things I was taught as a young Jesuit was never to debate an incorrect premise. ADA compliance is not a debatable issue.

It is the law and, let me repeat, there are *no excuses* for not living up to it.

Business, states and local governments must do whatever they have to. We rejected excuses in other civil rights fights and we reject them now.

Some of the other main issues on our list of priorities are parity for mental health, employment, and personal attendant services.

As a person with epilepsy, I have a strong identification with people who have "hidden disabilities." They are in some ways the most discriminated against and the least understood of all Americans with disabilities.

By definition, universal coverage must include people with psychiatric problems and it must include parity for mental health.

No legislation that excludes the health needs of 40 million Americans deserves to be called "universal." How can we cut out nearly one-sixth of the population and pretend to call it "universal" coverage?

We can't ignore these 40 million Americans and we won't abandon them.

> *"Complete victory will not have been won until we have total support for the principles embodied in ADA."*

If we allow them to be forgotten in the fight for health reform, we will have bought benefits for ourselves at the price of our pride and the sacrifice of our principles.

We can't do that and we won't.

Another "must" in real health care reform is personal assistance services for the severely disabled.

During the teleconferences, one participant said it all when he said: "ADA doesn't mean much when you can't get out of bed by yourself." I can't say it better than that.

The need for personal assistance services has not escaped President Clinton. He feels very strongly about it and has publicly said so.

Lastly, but as important as any other is the problem of employment. Millions of Americans with disabilities don't have a job and dim prospects for employment.

Although we represent nearly 20 percent of the total population, we account for only 4.3 percent of the workforce.

The overall unemployment rate for people with disabilities is nearly 17 percent.

That's close to three times the national average, and it's worse—much worse—for people with severe disabilities. Nearly two-thirds are without jobs and unable to support themselves.

We've got to fix that!

Changing Attitudes

In closing, I want to take a moment to talk about attitudes and the need for building public support for our objectives. In my view, it's even more important to change attitudes than it is to change laws.

Congress can pass laws 'til the cows come home, but real change comes from a change of heart.

Legislation that captures the spirit of the times creates a tailwind that can bring about the desired change faster than would otherwise be possible. But law only defines public policy, it does not assure its acceptance or practice.

ADA is now on the books. It is the law of the land, and it *will* be enforced.

President Clinton gave me his personal assurance of this when he asked me to chair the President's Committee.

His leadership counts for a great deal in our fight for equality because our struggle has moved from the legislative arena to a new battleground—one where we hold the moral high ground.

Discrimination has no place in America. It is morally unacceptable and personally reprehensible to most Americans.

We've made great progress, but complete victory will not have been won until we have total support for the principles embodied in ADA.

Not just because the law says so, but because it is the right thing to do.

Not just because you can be fined or sued for noncompliance, but because discrimination is an evil the American people will not tolerate.

At heart, our fight against discrimination is not just about tearing down walls or widening doorways. It has a much deeper meaning. In a larger sense, it is a statement about who we are and what kind of a country we are.

And it is more than just a fight for the rights of people with disabilities. It is a struggle for the soul of America and the empowerment of *all* Americans.

In a White House ceremony [in 1994], President Clinton expressed a thought about empowerment that I want to share with you. I think it will make you proud.

His words to a group of disability leaders were: "When you strip it all away, what we're really trying to do is empower the families of this country to live in dignity, to work in dignity, and to fulfill themselves. And in a strange way," he continued, "this is a battle that the disability community may be able to lead for the rest of America."

What he was saying is that no one understands hunger more than a hungry man and no one values justice more than someone who has suffered discrimination.

Let me end now . . . by posing two questions. Who are we? And why are we here?

We know who we are. We are citizens of the United States, the nation's largest minority, and a force with the power to bring about meaningful change for ourselves and future generations.

We are here because we understand that by working together we can make this a better country for ourselves and all Americans—a country that truly offers liberty and justice for all.

ADA Regulations Are Reasonable and Effective

by Janet Reno and Dick Thornburgh

About the authors: Janet Reno is the attorney general of the United States under the Clinton administration. Dick Thornburgh was the U.S. attorney general under the Bush administration.

Today [July 26, 1995], America celebrates the fifth anniversary of the Americans with Disabilities Act, the ADA. It is a good time to step back and examine a record of substantial achievement. Already, barriers to the full participation of people with disabilities are coming down—in grocery stores, restaurants, and hotels, in government buildings, banks and movie theaters.

Brightening a Bleak Picture

In 1990, before the ADA became law, people with disabilities often could not get a job, ride a city bus, or go to a restaurant or store. These barriers imposed staggering costs on the country. In signing the ADA, President George Bush estimated that each year federal, state and local governments spent almost $200 billion to support people with disabilities.

When it passed the law, Congress found that an overwhelming majority of individuals with disabilities lived in isolation and dependence. And it recognized that when store owners or employers excluded people because of their disabilities, civil rights laws were simply inadequate to redress this discrimination.

Thanks to the ADA, this bleak picture is beginning to brighten. The nation's six million private businesses and 80,000 state and local governments are making their services accessible to disabled people.

To a great extent, these outstanding results are a testament to the approach the Justice Department—in both Republican and Democratic administrations—has taken to enforcing the ADA. Our top priority has been to encourage voluntary compliance. We have geared the department's efforts toward education—providing technical assistance and information to help businesses and local governments comply with the act in easy, cost-effective ways. We have turned away from fringe issues and focused on the core principles of the act: equal access to goods and services that are necessary to daily life. And we have sought to use the ADA's enforcement tools—litigation and civil penalties—only as a resort against those who thumb their noses at the law.

Misleading Criticisms

Readers of the *Wall Street Journal*'s editorial page frequently hear a different story about the ADA. Although a Harris poll, commissioned by the National Organization on Disability, found that the overwhelming majority of business leaders support the act, some journalistic naysayers have charged that the law imposes unreasonable burdens. They mischaracterize the ADA by implying that it requires businesses to spend outrageous sums removing barriers almost overnight.

These criticisms miss the mark. The ADA's requirements provide flexibility to business and government. The ADA strikes a carefully calibrated balance between the rights of people with disabilities and the legitimate concerns of business and government, including cost. It merely codifies common sense.

For example, businesses must remove architectural barriers in existing facilities only when this goal is "readily achievable," that is, only when it can be done "without much difficulty or expense." What may not be readily achievable for a small business this year may well be achievable if profits improve next year. And the ADA encourages low-cost ways to solve a problem. Restaurants do not have to provide menus in braille; waiters can read them to blind customers. A business located on the second floor of an older building need not install an elevator; it would be enough to offer curbside service to customers with disabilities.

> *"The ADA strikes a carefully calibrated balance between the rights of people with disabilities and the legitimate concerns of business and government."*

Critics also charge that the ADA requires extensive renovation of all state and local government buildings. Again, they don't understand the law. The ADA requires all government *programs*, not all government *buildings*, to be accessible. Local governments need not do anything that would result in an undue financial burden. A town library, for example, need not provide elevators to reach upper floors, so long as librarians are available to retrieve books for patrons who use wheelchairs.

Litigation Is Rare

Finally, some claim that the ADA is harming businesses by subjecting them to lawsuits by people without real disabilities. But litigation under the act has been rare. The Justice Department and the Equal Employment Opportunity Commission, together, have averaged fewer than 25 suits a year between 1990 and 1995. A Justice Department review revealed about 650 ADA cases nationwide. Whether you compare these numbers to the total number of non-ADA cases in federal courts (about 850,000) or the number of employers covered by the act (about 650,000), one thing is clear: The ADA has not resulted in a flood of litigation.

Further, the ADA does not require employers to hire anyone who is not qualified for the job. An employee or job applicant may not succeed in claiming discrimination under the ADA unless he or she meets all of the requirements of the job and can perform its essential functions. The act simply demands that employers provide "reasonable accommodation" for otherwise qualified workers. Experience shows that most accommodations can be made without difficulty and at little or no cost. A study commissioned by Sears indicates that of 436 reasonable accommodations provided by the company, 69% cost nothing, 28% cost less than $1,000 and only 3% cost more than $1,000.

> *"The ADA has not resulted in a flood of litigation."*

Most people in the business community understand that the ADA has been good for business; it has expanded the markets served by most establishments and opened the doors to productive people with disabilities, all at a minimal cost. We are committed to making the ADA's goals a reality, to give Americans with disabilities an equal chance to participate in all this nation has to offer.

The ADA Can Benefit Businesses

by Mary Lord

About the author: *Mary Lord is an assistant managing editor for* U.S. News & World Report.

Business owners from beauticians to restaurateurs are in a sweat. On July 26, 1992, the provisions of the Americans with Disabilities Act kick in, and federal hot lines are being swamped by calls from concerned managers.

While few employers quarrel with the ADA's aim of integrating some 43 million disabled Americans into the workplace, many are uncertain about their precise obligations in achieving it. Can companies be sued if they fail to install elevators or undertake other costly renovations? What if reassigning a disabled employee violates union seniority rules? To anxious retailers like Mike Madison, who is trying to determine whether he must build ramps and new restrooms in his Madison's Home Furnishings stores, in Boise and Nampa, Idaho, the law seems maddeningly vague. "I'd like to accommodate everyone," he says, "but not to the detriment of my business."

Compliance Can Be Easy and Inexpensive

Phil Kosak, co-founder of Carolina Fine Snack Foods in Greensboro, N.C., isn't worried. In 1988, chronic absenteeism and carelessness nearly destroyed the firm just as it landed a lucrative contract to supply gourmet pork skins for the Republican National Convention. Instead of closing shop, Kosak hired a disabled man whose exemplary performance inspired the rest of the work force into shaping up. Today, half the firm's 18 employees have impairments—a track record that helped Carolina Fine Snack Foods early in 1992 to become the first small business to win accolades from the President's Committee on Employment of People with Disabilities. "Any manager who does not look first for a disabled person," says Kosak, "is leaving gold sitting on the back porch."

When it comes to complying with the ADA, most employers expect to pay a fortune, not find one. Passed virtually unopposed in 1990 over the protests of small business, the law prohibits discrimination against individuals with infirmities ranging from AIDS and epilepsy to paraplegia and schizophrenia. It also compels companies with 25 or more employees to make "reasonable accommodations" for qualified workers and job applicants with impairments. Another set of provisions, which took effect in January 1992, requires any enterprise that serves the public to improve the accessibility of such areas as store aisles, health clubs, even doctors' waiting rooms.

ADA experts argue that employers actually have great flexibility because of the statute's ambiguities. "I tell businesses they've got to use common sense," says Liz Savage, a sight-impaired attorney and training director for the Disability Rights Education and Defense Fund in Washington, D.C. "If I sued every hotel that didn't have a large-print phone list in the room, I'd be spending all my time in litigation. Life is tough enough."

"Any manager who does not look first for a disabled person . . . is leaving gold sitting on the back porch."

Contrary to their worst fears, business owners find that compliance can prove cheap and easy. For Sally Tholl, owner of the Step Five Design beauty salon in Ballston Spa, N.Y., it means sending someone out to assist cancer patients into the shop. Instead of splurging on Braille menus, which fewer than 20 percent of all sight-impaired Americans can read, restaurants can have a waiter read the menu aloud. Cup dispensers provide an inexpensive alternative to lowering drinking fountains for wheelchair-bound employees, while simply insulating exposed hot-water pipes under bathroom sinks allows paraplegics to wash up without scalding their legs. Indeed, according to a survey by the Job Accommodation Network, one of several federally funded ADA clearinghouses, 31 percent of all modifications cost nothing and two thirds can be done for under $500.

Of course, many businesses spend more—a lot more. Alan Armstrong, owner of the Tiffany Dining Place restaurant in Blue Bell, Pa., has hired architects to devise ways of improving accessibility. Modifications include widened doors in the newly renovated, $13,000 powder room, plus a grab bar in the men's toilet. But because the corridors are too short and the ceilings too low, building a ramp into the dining room seems infeasible. For now, customers are wheeled through the kitchen. "We've tried to do everything as environmentally and as politically correct as we can," says Armstrong. "But in this market, you can't afford everything."

Nor does the law demand it. The ADA explicitly makes exceptions for "undue hardship," for instance, while tax credits and deductions are available to help defray costs. Employers need not compromise safety standards either—or even give preference to a job candidate with a disability. "This is not a quota statute or an affirmative-action statute," assures Jonathan Mook, a law partner at Ogletree, Deakins, Nash, Smoak & Stewart in Washington, D.C., and author of an ADA litigation guide. "It's a totally interactive process between people with disabilities, employers and employees."

Improved Performance

Carolina Fine Snack Foods' experience demonstrates just how profitable that dialogue can prove. Before owner Kosak hired David Bruton, a sight-impaired man with severe learning disabilities who showed up at a local job fair, personnel problems were sapping the bottom line. Employees sometimes showed up drunk—if at all. Kosak found himself replacing warehouse hands every three weeks. Productivity was dismal, with miscounts and sloppy shipments the norm. "We were at our wits' end just trying to maintain a basic, semi-skilled work force," recalls Kosak.

David Bruton changed all that. Armed with a large-number calculator, which he brought himself, he kept track of outbound freight more accurately than had any previous able-bodied monitor. He greeted customers, established rapport and improved the customers' view of the company. Such diligence prompted other employees to spruce up their performance. Efficiency zoomed. Absenteeism plunged to almost zero as morale soared; the personnel director even taught herself sign language.

The bottom-line lesson was not lost on Kosak, who subsequently hired eight other disabled individuals. "There are still problems, but they are trivial compared with what I had before," he says.

As Carolina Fine Snack Foods learned, adjustments need not prove burdensome. Most simply entailed a little ingenuity and some extra training time. For instance, Kosak's learning-impaired employees have difficulty counting. To enable such workers to load the proper number of snack packs into a carton, Kosak simply shows them how a carton full of bags looks, and they are able to learn by imitation. Forms are simplified so that mentally disabled workers can keep track of inventory. "Employers are just afraid of taking the time to be a little bit creative," says Kosak.

> *"31 percent of all modifications cost nothing and two thirds can be done for under $500."*

Several surveys bear that out. A study conducted in June 1992 by the labor-law firm Jackson, Lewis, Schnitzler & Krupman found that 71 percent of the companies polled had set aside no funds for compliance. Of firms with more than 500 employees contacted in April by Buck Consultants, the New York–based benefits experts, just slightly more than half had reviewed or modified such personnel-selection criteria as employment tests.

Aids for Businesses

To assuage corporate concerns and ease compliance, the government has earmarked more than $8 million to establish training programs, hot lines and information clearinghouses. Response time may be slow, however. The Equal Employment Opportunity Commission, the lead enforcer of the ADA workplace provisions, currently fields more than 1,000 requests a day for publications (compared with 55 each day in 1991), and is struggling to whittle down its response time to four days.

Community groups that represent the disabled and trade associations also can provide a wealth of ideas on modifications. The Building Owners and Managers Association International in Washington, D.C., for example, has boiled 315 pages of regulations into a 325-item checklist of physical alterations. The Council of Better Business Bureaus in Arlington, Va., in addition to tracking down scammers who charge high fees for phony ADA certification, developed inexpensive compliance tip sheets for six industries, including retail outlets and fitness clubs. The Council also plans to offer mediation services to give employers and disabled employees an alternative means of settling discrimination complaints.

> *"The ADA explicitly makes exceptions for 'undue hardship.'"*

Though the law does not require them to go out and recruit, business owners can tap local agencies for talent as well. Many of the 6,000 disabled individuals hired by Pizza Hut since 1985 were aggressively recruited at vocational and rehabilitation centers.

Changing Mindsets

For all the brouhaha over physical modifications, it is the psychological adjustments required under the ADA—from application procedures to employment practices—that could prove the bigger legal challenge. For instance, simply giving a telephone number to call in a want ad may discriminate against individuals with hearing or speech impairments; ADA experts advise giving applicants the option to write for interviews. Du Pont, considered one of the country's most sensitive employers, changed its rules to allow new hires to use any photo identification instead of a driver's license, since that would exclude people with sight impairments, cerebral palsy or a host of other disabilities.

Many adjustments are less obvious. Under the ADA, a boss who tries to fire a diabetic for eating on the job risks trouble; if food poses a health or safety problem, the company can allow for breaks and offer a separate room for snacking. Employers cannot inquire into an applicant's past treatment for alcohol abuse— although drug testing remains permissible. Even the legal profession has had its fingers rapped; a lawyer with learning disabilities won the right to take the New York bar examination in a separate room and over four days instead of two.

Business owners may have a thorny time trying to determine whether a job applicant's health can keep him from performing essential tasks. The ADA forbids employers from asking about a job applicant's disabilities—even if they are germane to the job. Thus, a warehouse operator would be on safer legal ground to inquire if a prospective stevedore can lift 100 pounds rather than quizzing him on back problems. Companies also cannot refuse to hire an individual for fear his disability, or a family member's, will boost the cost of the firm's health insurance. However, an employer need not bolster that individual's benefits package or make special allowances for someone caring for a sick spouse.

Ultimately, the courts will have to settle many of the compliance questions now troubling employers. But if Carolina Fine Snack Foods' experience is any indication, lawyers don't have to be the only group to profit.

The ADA Can Prevent Discrimination by Insurance Companies

by Monica E. McFadden

About the author: *Monica E. McFadden is a Chicago-based lawyer.*

John McGann has AIDS. After discovering the nature of his illness, his employer alters his health insurance policy to reduce his lifetime coverage for AIDS-related care to $5,000, while maintaining the million-dollar limit for coverage for all other health conditions. Is this legal?

Harry Smith has insulin-dependent diabetes, which is under excellent control. He applies for individual health insurance and marks "yes" to the question about diabetes on the application. Without ever reviewing his medical records or talking to his physician, the company denies coverage. In a letter, the insurance provider identifies the diabetes as the express reason for its decision. Can the company do that?

Joan Doe has breast cancer, which is in remission. She changes employers. Her new employer's insurance company excludes coverage for any preexisting medical condition. The insurer refuses to cover her yearly mammograms, although it covers them for all other employees. Is this legal?

Insurance Discrimination

Before passage of the Americans with Disabilities Act (ADA), the answer to each of these questions was a resounding "yes." Insurance discrimination based on a person's disability was subject to a rational review standard. So long as an employer or an insurer had some rational basis for the discrimination, it was legal. In *McGann v. H & H Music Co.*, for example, the court accepted the employer's reasoning that providing equal coverage for AIDS and other conditions would bankrupt the health plan. No evidence was produced, just the employer's representation.

Monica E. McFadden, "The Americans with Disabilities Act: Fighting Discrimination," *Trial*, September 1995. Copyright The Association of Trial Lawyers of America. Reprinted with permission of *Trial* magazine.

The ADA has the potential to change this. When President George Bush signed the act into law, he called it "the world's first comprehensive declaration of equality for people with disabilities." It is a unique and powerful tool that can be used to challenge blatant disability-based distinctions in insurance that have harmed people unfairly for many years. Just as race-based distinctions are illegal under the Civil Rights Act, disability-based distinctions in insurance should be illegal under the ADA.

Unfortunately, nothing is ever that easy. In drafting the ADA, Congress added language that has led the insurance industry to argue that it can continue to use pre-ADA underwriting formulas based solely on disability to justify refusal, higher premiums, or lower coverage. The legal battle in this arena is just beginning. It will be won or lost in U.S. courtrooms, by trial lawyers prepared to use the new law to challenge this invalid presumption of insurers.

Current Practices

The current regulatory structure for insurance includes the Employee Retirement Income Security Act (ERISA), which governs employee benefit programs provided by large employers, and state insurance law. Under ERISA as it was interpreted before the ADA, employers could use any rating or administration factors they wished, even disability, as long as they could show some rational basis for their choice and that the choice was not proscribed by some other federal discrimination law.

Under state law, underwriters may use any factors to set rates, premiums, or eligibility, as long as members of the same class who have substantially the same characteristics are treated similarly. State law, however, must bow to federal discrimination law when the two conflict.

Most insurers and employers currently use factors the ADA defines as disabilities to limit the scope, duration, or eligibility requirements for their plans. Common examples include limits on benefits for diabetes, arthritis, heart disease, drug addiction and alcoholism, and preexisting condition exclusions or limitations on coverage.

> *"Blatant disability-based distinctions in insurance . . . have harmed people unfairly for many years."*

In addition, insurers underwrite risks in many plans, charging higher rates or refusing entry to plans if the risk is perceived to be too high. They do this through the use of statistics, by making actuarial assessments designed to balance risk and cost. The principle is that through record keeping and statistics, the insurers are able to prove to regulators that certain conditions cost considerably more and therefore warrant higher premiums or complete exclusion.

The recent debate on health care reform and previous debates on insurance practices have called those formulas and data into question, however. Advocates have accused insurers of using outmoded data and inaccurate formulas and of failing to take into account the investment value of premiums. Advocates also point to recruitment practices designed to select lower risk individuals and to churning practices that end coverage as soon as payouts must occur. It will be on these issues that ADA discrimination claims will be won or lost.

ADA Regulations

The ADA has several titles and sections that cover insurance, insurers, and insurance practices. An understanding of the statutory language, construction, legislative history, and regulations is vital to beginning any insurance discrimination analysis.

Title I prohibits discrimination in employment against a qualified person with a disability. A person with a disability is considered qualified if the person satisfies the job requirements and can perform essential functions with or without reasonable accommodation.

The ADA broadly defines a person with a disability as one who (a) has a physical or mental impairment that substantially limits one or more major life activities, (b) has a record of such impairment, or (c) is regarded as having such an impairment. This definition covers diverse conditions such as blindness, mobility restrictions, obesity, AIDS, alcoholism, and heart disease.

> *"Under the ADA, a person with a disability cannot be denied insurance or be subject to different terms or conditions of insurance."*

Significantly, Title I specifically bars discrimination in employee compensation and in other terms, conditions, and privileges of employment, such as health insurance. Nor can an employer contract with a provider of fringe benefits who subjects employees to discrimination on the basis of disability.

Title III bars discrimination in any public accommodation. Public accommodation is defined to include insurance offices and any services provided in those offices. Title III is particularly pertinent to insurance because it expressly forbids denial of participation, inequality in participation, or provision of separate benefits to a person on the basis of disability. It also prohibits using eligibility criteria that screen out people with disabilities, and it requires corrective action where necessary to ensure that they are not discriminated against.

The ADA's legislative history supports directly applying the statute to all insurance and employee benefits cases. The House and Senate committee reports specifically name insurance as a covered employment benefit under Title I.

Referring to Title III, the legislative history states: "Under the ADA, a person with a disability cannot be denied insurance or be subject to different terms or conditions of insurance based on disability alone, if the disability does not pose increased risks."

Of vital importance to an insurance discrimination suit, the ADA bars both disparate treatment (differentiations based directly on disability) and disparate impact (differentiations having the effect of discrimination based on disability, which tend to screen out people with disabilities). The act explicitly includes disparate impact "to ensure that the legislative mandate to end discrimination does not ring hollow."

Reasonable Accommodations

Congress was not unaware, however, that the ADA's broad goals inevitably conflict with the realities of accommodating disabilities. To resolve these conflicts, Congress created what I call a "cost-justification test," which does not appear in other civil rights legislation. It most likely will have a direct impact on insurance discrimination suits.

Under this test, an accommodation that would create an undue hardship for the business or fundamentally alter the nature of the product is a defense to a claim of discrimination. To protect the disabled person, however, the definitions of "reasonable accommodation" and "undue hardship" require providers to prove that they would incur significant effort and expense before they can successfully claim these defenses.

Whether the effort to provide reasonable accommodation qualifies as unduly burdensome depends on the financial and structural resources of the covered entity. Obviously, this defense will be seen often in insurance discrimination cases.

The ADA also contains a section specific to insurance—Title V, §501(c), which states

> Insurance—Titles I through IV of this act shall not be construed to prohibit or restrict—
>
> (1) an insurer, hospital or medical service company, health maintenance organization, or any agent, or entity that administers benefit plans, or similar organizations from underwriting risks, classifying risks, or administering such risks that are based on or not inconsistent with state law; or
>
> (2) a person or organization covered by this act from establishing, sponsoring, observing or administering the terms of a bona fide benefit plan that are based on underwriting risks, classifying risks, or administering such risks that are based on or not inconsistent with state law; or
>
> (3) a person or organization covered by this act from establishing, sponsoring, observing or administering the terms of a bona fide benefit plan that is not subject to state laws that regulate insurance.
>
> Paragraphs (1), (2) and (3) shall not be used as a subterfuge to evade the purposes of Title I and III.

The legislative history shows Congress added §501(c) to clarify that it did not intend for the act to "disrupt the current nature of insurance underwriting or the current regulatory structure for self-insured employers or of the insurance industry." This language will be hotly contested in the ensuing legal battles.

Congress also made clear, however, that it did not intend for all current practices to continue unabated. The legislative history interpreting §501(c) states:

> While a plan which limits certain kinds of coverage based on classification of risk would be allowed under this section, the plan may not refuse to insure, or refuse to continue to insure or limit the amount, extent, or kind of coverage available to an individual, or charge a different rate for the same coverage solely because of a physical or mental impairment, except where the refusal, limitation, or rate differential is based on sound actuarial principles or is related to actual or reasonably anticipated experience.

This language should serve as the blueprint for trial lawyers when prosecuting insurance cases. The issue is whether insurers can prove that the disability discrimination is warranted by factual proof. Arguably, as discussed above, most cannot. If they cannot, the distinctions are arguably "subterfuge" to evade the purposes of the act and are illegal.

Proving Subterfuge

"Subterfuge" is not defined in the ADA. However, under both the legislative history of the act and the guidelines of agencies responsible for implementing it, certain practices constitute subterfuge and therefore discrimination. These include
- refusing to employ someone because the employer's current insurance does not cover the disability;
- refusing to provide insurance simply because it will be more expensive;
- denying coverage without an independent actuarial analysis of the risk;
- making an insurance office inaccessible to avoid applications from people with disabilities (for example, putting the only office in a third-story walk-up); or
- implementing preexisting condition clauses or other clauses that result in disparate impact.

For example, the Equal Employment Opportunity Commission (EEOC) states that a plan that excludes from coverage any preexisting blood disorders for 18 months is presumptively discriminatory. The reason is that the exclusion would affect only a discrete group of related disabilities, such as leukemia and hemophilia.

> *"The beauty of the ADA ... is the burden of proof it puts on the insurer, employer, or administrator."*

Under this guideline, certain cases are easy to prove. These are the blatant discrimination cases in which a disability is clearly being used as a screening device independent of any evaluation. Examples are those cases, similar to *McGann,* where caps are placed on benefits for HIV or AIDS-related illnesses while other illnesses continue to be provided higher levels of coverage. The EEOC has vigorously pursued these cases and has argued successfully that they are per se discrimination.

Other cases will, however, require significant investigation and factual preparation, such as Harry Smith's, discussed earlier. Both the EEOC and the Department of Justice recognize that disability-related distinctions are acceptable if they are justified by the risks or costs associated with the disability. Employers and insurers are already realizing that the cost-justification test provides them with a potentially powerful defense. More and more will try to use this defense to counter discrimination claims.

The beauty of the ADA, however, is the burden of proof it puts on the insurer, employer, or administrator. Under standard insurance law, virtually any association between disability and increased cost is considered sufficient to justify discrimination. But under the ADA, insurers and plan administrators may not use actuarial or experience data that is outdated; inaccurate; or based on myths, fears, stereotypes, or false assumptions.

If the insurer or employer raises the defense that it would be an undue hardship to cover the disability, it must be prepared to open its data banks and policy manuals to discovery by plaintiffs and juries. In Harry Smith's case, the company would have to show why the cost of care for a controlled diabetic is an unacceptable risk.

The plaintiff must be prepared to actively pursue discovery. This requires analysis and review of statistical formulas, financial books and materials, and medical and scientific proofs. The plaintiff must also explain their relevance to the jury.

For example, consider the argument that providing care for HIV or AIDS is more expensive than for other conditions. This could easily be countered by comparing the cost of care for terminal breast cancer and making arguments about similar life expectancies.

Harry Smith's diabetes-based discrimination case can be countered by using data from a 1995 national study showing that when blood sugar levels are kept under strict control, the potential complications from diabetes, such as cardiac failure and eye disease, are significantly reduced. The plaintiff must be prepared, however, to do the necessary research and obtain the expert assistance needed to make this case.

Insurance Coverage for AIDS

McGann is the pre-ADA case in which the employer unilaterally put a $5,000 cap on AIDS benefits but let stand a $1 million limit on all other illnesses. The employer argued successfully that to cover AIDS to the same extent as other illnesses would bankrupt his plan, harming his other employees. No proof beyond his self-serving assertion was offered or required.

Under the ADA, both the evidentiary standards and the outcome of this case would be significantly different. Remember that under the ADA, differentiations on the basis of disability are permitted only if (1) the validity of the differentiation can be documented by recent data or (2) the cost of creating a classification, premium, or benefit program not based on disability would be unduly burdensome or would fundamentally alter the nature of the insurance or benefit product.

The plaintiff's prima facie case would consist of the following elements:

- evidence that a person has a disability but is otherwise qualified for the insurance or benefit;
- evidence that the employer or insurer knows that disability is being used as a rating factor; and
- evidence that the employer or insurer discriminated against the person by making a decision about eligibility requirements, pricing, or administration of benefits based on the person's disability.

If this standard is applied to *McGann* post-ADA, McGann would clearly meet the burden of proof. As a person with a disability (AIDS), he is qualified to get insurance through the group plan because he is an employee of H & H Music. His employer reduced the benefits offered for AIDS, which subjected McGann to differential treatment based on his disability. The employer stipulated that the decision was made with the knowledge of McGann's illness and the impact the change in coverage would have on him.

The burden of proof would then shift to the employer or insurer, either of whom could defend the reduction by demonstrating that

- documentation exists showing that the use of the disability to classify or rate that person is related to actual or reasonably anticipated experience or is based on sound actuarial principles; or
- the cost of creating a classification, premium, or benefit program not based on disability would be unduly burdensome or would fundamentally alter the nature of the product.

Here, H & H Music's alleged inability to preserve benefits for other employees while continuing to cover AIDS might qualify as an affirmative defense. It would, however, require a significant factual inquiry. H & H Music would have to show at minimum that (1) AIDS is an expensive condition; (2) maintaining its current benefit plan, which offers equal benefits for all conditions, would be unduly burdensome; and (3) providing AIDS benefits would virtually bankrupt the plan.

> *"Under the ADA, insurers . . . may not use actuarial or experience data that is . . . based on myths, fears, stereotypes, or false assumptions."*

The outcome of the case would depend on the proof submitted by H & H Music. Arguably, the company would be unable to meet this burden. According to the medical literature, the estimated average lifetime costs for an AIDS patient range from $25,000 to $147,000.

But there are other conditions employees may suffer that are as expensive, if not more expensive, than AIDS. For example, according to one set of researchers, the average cost of treatment for breast cancer ranges from $36,100 for standard chemotherapy to $89,700 for an autologous bone marrow transplant. Therefore, it would be difficult for H & H to justify restricting one condition while not restricting others.

Given the facts of this case, McGann would win. The same should be true for many discrimination plaintiffs. The challenge will be, as former Association of Trial Lawyers of America President Harry Philo says, to make sure that the case law in this area "is settled right." This is our challenge as trial lawyers representing people who are the consumers of insurance—to make sure the law in this area is developed and settled right.

It is a challenge worth assuming.

ADA Regulations Are Unreasonable and Ineffective

by Edward L. Hudgins

About the author: *Edward L. Hudgins is the director of regulatory studies at the Cato Institute, a libertarian public policy research organization. He is also the senior editor of* Regulation, *a quarterly periodical published by the institute.*

The Americans with Disabilities Act (ADA), which was signed into law on July 26, 1990, passed the U.S. Senate with only six nay votes and the House of Representatives with only 28. The bill had the strong support of President George Bush. . . .

The ADA was inspired in part by a desire to protect disabled Americans from hiring discrimination the same way civil rights legislation purports to protect racial and ethnic minorities. In fact, the ADA is one of the worst cases of the Bush-era reregulation of the economy. It runs contrary to . . . sound policy principles because

- It devalues property by restricting use without paying the owners any compensation;
- It adds to the costs for enterprises to do business and for state and local governments to provide services, often with few, if any, offsetting benefits;
- Its requirements that state and local governments provide special facilities, many of which go under- or unutilized, are prototypical unfunded mandates.

The ADA suffers from other shortcomings as well:

- Its vague and contradictory definitions constitute irresponsible delegation of power by Congress to the courts and officials that must interpret the ADA's meaning;
- It has unleashed a plague of needless lawsuits; and
- In some ways it harms the very group it means to help: disabled Americans.

Excerpted from Edward L. Hudgins, "Handicapping Freedom: The Americans with Disabilities Act," *Regulation*, no. 2, 1995. Reprinted by permission of the Cato Institute.

The ADA puts the rhetoric of both Republicans and Democrats to the test. By the Republicans' own criteria, it never should have been passed, certainly not in its current form. The Democrats profess to favor a "common-sense" approach to regulation, but the ADA constitutes the abrogation of common sense. If Congress is serious about lifting the regulatory burden from the economy, it must consider major changes in, if not outright repeal of, the ADA. And if Congress is to undo the damage already done by the act, it should consider paying reparations to cover the costs that individuals, private establishments, and enterprises have suffered under the ADA's provisions.

Two Types of Civil Rights Policies

Few would disagree that, unlike able-bodied citizens, Americans with real physical disabilities face special challenges as they attempt to earn their livings and enjoy their lives. It is also understandable that policymakers would want to ease the burdens that disabled Americans face.

President Bush and his supporters in Congress promoted the ADA as a civil rights law. They argued that just as legislation in the 1960s sought to eliminate hiring discrimination and remove restrictions that kept blacks off city buses or out of private restaurants and hotels, the ADA would do the same for the handicapped. But there are two types of civil rights policies. One type requires that governments refrain from actions based, for example, on racial considerations. When applied to private behavior, such policies generally do not tend to require individuals to take positive actions, nor do they impose direct costs on individuals. Public facilities incurred no additional direct costs by accommodating all customers regardless of race. Nor were there major indirect costs, for example, from whites boycotting integrated establishments. Further, a business that hires the best job applicant regardless of race is following a wise and profitable practice, and certainly does not incur any additional direct costs.

> *"Congress . . . must consider major changes in, if not outright repeal of, the ADA."*

The other type of civil rights policy, based on a positive conception of rights, requires certain actions by governments or private individuals and can impose direct costs on them as well, often in the name of creating a level playing field. Hiring quotas and affirmative action, for example, can require businesses to employ a certain percentage of workers from a given racial or ethnic group, whether those individuals meet the employment needs of an enterprise or not.

The ADA is a civil rights law of the latter type, based on a positive conception of rights. It requires local governments and private enterprises to pay the costs of accommodation out of their own pockets.

Part of the philosophy behind the ADA is that disabled Americans should not be helped in ways that separate them from other citizens. Rather, to the greatest extent possible, Americans with disabilities should enjoy equal access to the same public places as other Americans; and in the workplace, employers should make reasonable accommodations for disabled workers. But in light of Republican calls for a cost-benefit rule to be applied to new regulations, the definitions of terms such as "reasonable" and the like, found throughout the ADA, take on added importance. As shall be seen below, in practice the ADA has strayed far from the common-sense approach.

Principal Provisions

The principal provisions of the ADA are summarized below.

Title I prohibits discrimination by public or private employers. Specifically, Title I, section 102 (a) of the ADA establishes that an employer cannot "discriminat[e] against a qualified individual with a disability because of the disability of such individual in regard to job application procedures, the hiring, advancement or discharge of employees, employment compensation, job training, and other terms, conditions, and privileges of employment."

> *"In practice the ADA has strayed far from the common-sense approach."*

A disabled individual is protected if he can perform the "essential functions" of a position. The ADA also requires employers to make "reasonable accommodations" for the disabled employee. Such accommodations include job restructuring; part-time or modified work schedules; reassignment to vacant positions when the disability is so severe that employees no longer qualify for the position for which they were originally hired; or provision of qualified readers or interpreters. The act specifies that employers shall not be guilty of discrimination if "reasonable accommodations" create an "undue hardship" for them, meaning that the action would require "significant difficulty and expense." Prior to an offer of employment, employers may not inquire about whether an applicant is disabled or about "the nature or severity of such disability."

Complaints involving Title I violations must be filed with the federal government's Equal Employment Opportunity Commission (EEOC). The employment provisions of the act took effect in mid-1992 for businesses of 25 or more employees, and were applied to establishments with as few as 15 workers as of July 1994. Originally, government action in response to complaints was supposed to be principally remedial, emphasizing correcting access problems—though equitable remedies could be imposed. Private damage awards were excluded in order to head off predatory lawsuits. But the 1991 Civil Rights Act amendments added to the ADA jury trials and damage awards of up to $300,000 for "pain and suffering." . . .

Types of Complaints

The ADA requires employers to make reasonable accommodations for employees with disabilities. But the specific accommodations mentioned in the act are anything but reasonable. For example, for an employer to provide qualified readers or interpreters—considered "reasonable" under the ADA—without regard to the employee's payscale, can be very costly. The facts indicate that by a cost-benefit standard, Title I has been less than successful.

An examination of the types of complaints under the ADA gives us some indication of the act's effectiveness. Between July 26, 1992 and March 31, 1995, some 45,053 ADA-based complaints were filed with the EEOC, a rate of about 15,000 annually. Of that number, only 4,806 complaints, or 10.7 percent of the total, concerned hiring discrimination.

Fully 22,834 ADA cases, or 50.7 percent of the total, dealt with dismissal of persons already employed. Failure to provide reasonable accommodation accounted for 11,819 cases, or 26.2 percent of the total.

"The ADA so far does not seem to be an efficient way to get the disabled 'mainstreamed' into the workforce."

Those numbers suggest that nearly 90 percent of those availing themselves of the ADA already are or have been in the workforce. In other words, the ADA so far does not seem to be an efficient way to get the disabled "mainstreamed" into the workforce.

Of the types of disabilities claimed in complaints to the EEOC, 8,738, or 19.4 percent, concerned back problems. Such suits are often combined with workers' compensation cases. In those cases, workers claiming to be unable to perform due to work-related injuries will also claim to be disabled, and therefore protected by the ADA.

Some 5,354 individuals, or 11.9 percent of those filing complaints, had neurological impairments, while 5,243 persons, or 11.6 percent, claimed emotional or psychological problems.

The blind, the deaf, and the motor-impaired—those typically thought of as "disabled"—make up only a fraction of those filing complaints. There were 3,500 people, 7.6 percent of the total, who required wheelchairs or had other difficulties with locomotion; 1,360, or 3 percent, were deaf or hearing impaired; and 1,257, or 2.8 percent, were blind or visually impaired.

Of the 45,043 cases filed, 24,494, or 54 percent, have been resolved. And of those, 46.1 percent were resolved through administrative closures, meaning, in most cases, that the complaining party failed to follow up sufficiently to make a complete complaint. Another 43.9 percent were thrown out for lacking reasonable cause. Those figures indicate that only a small portion of ADA employment complaints have merit. Of course, even if defendants avoid liabilities, they do not avoid the costs of defending themselves. . . .

Conceptual Problems

The employment provisions of the ADA contain a number of conceptual problems that could be expected to result in excessive costs and administrative burdens on employers seeking to comply with the act. . . .

Predicting Hardship. For an employer to judge whether he can make reasonable accommodation for a potential employee who is disabled, he must know what disabilities a job applicant has. But Title I, section 102 (c)(2)(A) of the ADA states that an employer "shall not conduct a medical examination or make inquiries of a job applicant as to whether such applicant is an individual with a disability or as to the nature or severity of such disability."

An employer might easily determine the effect of a disability and screen out those not qualified for a job by giving an applicant a test—for example, asking a wheelchair-bound individual to place a heavy box on a top shelf in a warehouse, if that were one of the essential functions of the available job. But a more difficult problem is how to determine future costs that might only become apparent after an applicant is hired. If he is not allowed to make inquiries, how can an employer know before the fact whether an employee will add an "undue hardship" or "substantial costs" to his business? And once an individual is hired, firing him because of a disability, no matter how costly that disability is to the business, virtually guarantees an ADA suit.

Job Inflexibility. Another problem with the ADA is that it impedes businesses' attempts to increase efficiency by increasing worker flexibility. For a decade or more the trend in American business has been towards more flexibility, allowing or expecting employees to do a number of tasks and to fill in wherever they are needed. But the ADA can hamper the honest efforts of businesses to operate more efficiently. For certain positions, it still might be easy to identify an "essential" function that the ADA would not adversely affect. For example, a large firm maintaining a large typing pool in which workers spend all day typing would not find its flexibility impaired by hiring individuals in wheelchairs. But forcing other enterprises, especially smaller ones, to limit disabled employees' work to "essential" functions could be a serious constraint.

Discrimination by Process. The ADA does not simply ban outright discrimination. Rather, in Title I, section 102 (b)(3)(A) it bans hiring practices "that have the effect of discrimination on the basis of disability." That suggests that application of the ADA will follow the pattern set by various civil rights laws. Even if no explicit discrimination exists, activists will see in the results that certain firms do not hire as many

> *"Connecticut attorney Patrick Shea estimates that the minimum legal bill for an ADA case is $10,000."*

disabled individuals as the activists believe is appropriate. Indeed, the link to abuses of civil rights law is a close one, since the 1991 Civil Rights Act amendments amended the ADA retroactively to allow collection for damages and jury trials. Activists can now claim that hiring practices have the "effect of discriminating." The burden does not rest upon the plaintiff or the government to prove discrimination; it rests on the employer to prove that he is innocent.

Chapter 1

A Wave of Lawsuits

Critics of the ADA claimed that the vague definitions of "reasonable accommodation" and other elements of the act would give rise to costly and ludicrous lawsuits. Unfortunately, those critics were correct. . . .

The current wave of lawsuits under the ADA creates four adverse effects. First, businesses will pay more to settle lawsuits against them under the ADA. It is difficult to obtain hard data concerning the costs because very often settlements are for undisclosed sums. But it can be assumed that in order to avoid high legal bills, employers often settle, even when they have a good chance to win in court. In addition, the bad press associated with being sued by a sympathetic plaintiff will often force settlement. . . .

> *"The ADA may cause employer hostility towards the disabled."*

A second adverse effect of the ADA is higher legal bills for enterprises to defend against lawsuits. Since an enterprise must absorb the costs of its legal bills even when it wins a case, those bills will add to the costs of doing business. Connecticut attorney Patrick Shea estimates that the minimum legal bill for an ADA case is $10,000. Minnesota ADA lawyer Tom Marshall puts settlement costs at around $75,000.

A third adverse effect of the ADA is higher insurance costs for those enterprises that do not self-insure. In cases in which employers provide health care insurance for workers, higher costs would likely come from the need to meet the special needs of the disabled. But insurance to cover some of the costs of lawsuits is an even more likely added expense.

Finally, and perhaps most tragically, the ADA may cause employer hostility towards the disabled. Before the ADA, many employers were inclined to hire handicapped individuals for jobs that would pose no major difficulties for them. Employers might reason that handicapped workers would be especially anxious to do good jobs, to prove themselves worthy of their tasks, to show that their disabilities are, in effect, no real handicap. McDonald's, for example, went out of its way before the enactment of the ADA to recruit mentally handicapped workers for its fast-food outlets.

But under the ADA the employer is more likely to see a handicapped applicant as a lawsuit waiting to happen. If a handicapped worker does not receive regular raises or promotions, is criticized for unsatisfactory performance, or must be dismissed, the employer knows that the lawsuit remedy is an open and likely option for the employee. Employers need only examine the record of years of race-based lawsuits under civil rights legislation, most of which were without merit.

Some employers may look for any way to avoid hiring a disabled worker. Few will ever express such intentions publicly, for fear of appearing insensitive to those with demonstrable disabilities. But just as there is enough off-the-record, anecdotal evidence to suggest that that is the case for hiring minorities, so it is becoming the case with the disabled. Other employers might hire a certain number of handicapped individuals and keep them on staff as tokens, no matter how inefficient they are; but that is hardly an attitude that will benefit the handicapped.

Title II of the ADA, which requires public facilities such as public buildings and transportation to be accessible to the disabled, is a prototypical unfunded mandate, imposing costs on state and local governments. Since the ADA is relatively new, good data on the costs are hard to come by. But what evidence there is suggests both the magnitude of the costs and the severity of the tradeoffs involved.

A Price-Waterhouse study issued in October 1993 for the National Association of Counties surveyed 125 counties, representing 25 percent of the American population, and extrapolated to determine the total cost of unfunded mandates. For the ADA, it estimated an annual cost of $293.7 million, with a five-year cost of $2.8 billion. But even that amount seems low when the costs to particular localities are considered. A U.S. Conference of Mayors study puts the overall cost for cities at $2.2 billion. While more empirical work needs to be done on costs, as states, counties, and cities begin to comply with the ADA's provisions, some examples suggest the magnitude of the costs.

• The city of Philadelphia lost a case protesting an ADA requirement that it put curb-cuts for wheelchairs on the corners of every street it resurfaces, not just renovated or newly built streets. Mayor Rendell fears that if the city is required to go back and alter curbs on every street resurfaced while the case was being fought, the cost could be as high as $140 million. Even if the number is high for Philadelphia, multiplying the cost nationwide for curb-cuts alone gives an idea of the costs of compliance.

It is obvious that any expenditure requires tradeoffs. Wages for Philadelphia's approximately 4,300 police officers are about $43,000 each in direct payroll costs annually, and perhaps as high as $60,000 with benefits. The $140 million that might be used for curb-cuts could hire 1,200 officers for a two-year period.

• The Good Hope Middle School in Cumberland Valley, Pennsylvania, is facing costs of between $5.8 million and $7.3 million in renovations to meet ADA requirements.

• An August 1993 report by the state of Ohio estimated that the costs

"Banks have been required to install braille instructions on drive-through automatic teller machines on the driver's side."

for conversions mandated by the ADA could be $311.5 million for its 4,000 state buildings, $148.3 million for public transit, and $119.2 million for state universities and colleges.

Attempts to "mainstream" the disabled by adapting public transportation add rigidities to the ways that localities can meet ADA standards, and thus increase the costs of meeting those standards. For example, cities of certain sizes with certain numbers of handicapped citizens might find it less costly to provide door to door limo service on call for the disabled. But the ADA mandates, for example, that all new buses be equipped with wheelchair lifts and that subways be retrofitted over time with elevators. Further, lifts and elevators break down, inconveniencing wheelchair users. Local officials often keep vans and other means of transportation available for those whose disabilities are so severe that they cannot use buses and subways. It makes more sense to allow localities the flexibility to devise their own transportation mixes. . . .

Mandating Unreasonable Accommodations

Title III of the ADA requires privately provided public accommodations to be accessible to the disabled. It applies to office buildings, stores, restaurants, theaters, and the like. Some evidence indicates that adjustment costs and difficulties could vary based on several factors. In California, a state that passed fairly stringent public accommodations laws in the 1980s, adjustments in many cases were not as costly as elsewhere, simply because many enterprises had already made the transition.

While accommodations under Title III are supposed to be "reasonable," some are nonsensical by any standard. For example, banks have been required to install braille instructions on drive-through automatic teller machines on the driver's side. Another case involved a Florida man with muscular dystrophy who is suing the Walt Disney World Marathon because he was denied a chance to compete in the wheelchair race. He had a motorized wheelchair, and the race was for manual wheelchairs.

The ADA has been especially costly for restaurants. Uncertainty concerning the definition of "reasonable accommodation" is the usual problem. For example, in 1993 a lawsuit against McDonald's Corp. and Burger King Corp. was filed on behalf of individuals with asthma. The suit sought to ban smoking in those fast-food restaurants. At the time both McDonald's and Burger King already had nonsmoking sections; but that was not sufficient for the activists. A lower court dismissed the suit, but on April 4, 1995, the Second U.S. Circuit Court of Appeals ruled that the case should go to trial. . . .

The ADA is a classic example of well-intentioned legislation that was so poorly thought through that it is now, and likely in the future will be, a major source of lawsuits and unnecessary costs to the private and public sector. The definition of "disabled" includes so many individuals as to make a mockery of those who truly suffer handicaps. The definition of "reasonable accommodation" is anything but reasonable. The lack of flexibility adds needlessly to compliance costs when other, less costly options are available. The ADA is, in effect, a national building code, justified in the name of civil rights. And often the disabled reap few, if any, benefits from such costly efforts. If Congress is serious about relieving the citizens of the current regulatory burden, it must have the courage to reexamine the ADA.

ADA Compliance Is Too Expensive

by Brian Doherty

About the author: *Brian Doherty is an assistant editor for* Reason, *a monthly libertarian periodical.*

The Americans with Disabilities Act's (ADA) total costs are impossible to estimate with certainty. All we can know about are individual cases, and even there most people don't want to talk. With a law that is usually triggered by activist complaints, says a restaurateur, "in a lot of cases someone is afraid that something they say is going to come back to them."

The law rewards "good faith" compliance, so it behooves any business owner or manager not to say anything publicly that might betray a lack of good faith toward the ADA or its application. Lawyers, pundits, consultants, city officials, trade group reps, even people forced to pay tens of thousands trying to obey the law, all emphasize they have no problem with the concept of the ADA, just the uncertainty and stringency of its application.

Trouble at the Barolo Grill

Restaurateur Blair Taylor isn't as sanguine about his experience with the ADA. He owns the Barolo Grill in Denver—"a very high profile, upscale, Jags-and-Rolls-Royces type of Italian restaurant in an expensive shopping district called Cherry Creek.". . .

Taylor is "a 40-year-old yuppieish kind of white guy. I'm a safe, wonderful target for these things." "These things" for Taylor mean nearly two years of legal conflicts with both the Justice Department (DOJ) and the city of Denver that ended up costing around $100,000 in construction and legal fees.

Taylor's troubles started in December 1992, just after opening the Grill, with a phone call from the DOJ. "Apparently they had been peering in during construction, and noticed we hadn't done some work we should have done. They told me they were investigating complaints for noncompliance," he says. He wasn't immediately responsive: "The first week of running a new restaurant isn't when you have a lot of free time." Taylor insists that he could take a walk from his restaurant and find 40 businesses in worse ADA shape than his was. He thinks he may have been under surveillance because of complaints against the former owner of a restaurant in the location, but "never can I get a specific answer from DOJ. They'll just say, 'No, Mr. Taylor was a horrible person.'"

Not exactly a horrible person, but DOJ civil rights lawyer Kate Nicholson, who worked on the Barolo case, does call Taylor "very difficult." She denies any malice or example-making, stressing that Taylor made continual promises to make changes by given dates and missed them all. DOJ isn't generally quick to sue, she says.

> *"At least $250,000 was spent to force a restaurant in Denver to comply [with ADA regulations]."*

DOJ was unhappy with the four-inch step up to the door of the Barolo Grill, even though parking valets would always be available to help wheelchair users over the hump. Justice Department enforcers also didn't like the 11-inch raised platform in the back of the Barolo, with nine tables in addition to the 17 on the main floor.

A ramp to the platform was built, destroyed, and then rebuilt in response to Justice's complaints. The first time the ramp wasn't long enough for DOJ's very detailed building standards. The ramp is now the requisite 11 feet long and 41 inches wide to navigate a 11-inch rise, costing Taylor three tables worth of space in his usually sold-out restaurant.

Local and Federal Rules Conflict

The front ramp created a whole new set of problems, since it violated Denver city ordinances and required variances. "I said, 'I promised the federal government I'd do this ASAP, and city law won't let me do it?'" says Taylor. "It was an eight-and-a-half month process through various city boards.

"The federal government at the same time are saying, 'Faster, faster.' They'll say Mr. Taylor went back on his word several times, but the city wouldn't let me keep my word." DOJ's Nicholson was uncertain of the details of Taylor's problems with the city. All she knew was, he was violating the law and wasn't quick enough to remedy things.

By February 1994 Taylor had city permits for his ramps, bathrooms, fire alarm, roof drainage, sanitary water waste management tests, new air systems, and strobe lighting—"a tremendous number of irrelevant things that were at bottom about putting in two ramps." The DOJ went ahead and sued anyway in April, since they still had some complaints.

"They're demanding a $50,000 fine, the maximum for a first-time offender. And the price tag to go into federal court is very expensive anyway. We're forced to go to a settlement conference. I say that I'm in complete compliance, and if I can just pay a fine I'd like to go home."

DOJ didn't agree. Its complaints included: The handrails on the entrance ramp had two more inches between them and the restaurant's window than the law allows; the restroom grab bar was mounted two-and-a-half inches too far from the back wall; carpeting ended two inches before the patio door; and the wine storage room didn't have a ramp to its door (which was also not wide enough).

DOJ's biggest complaint was the back alley exit ramp, insisted on by Denver as a fire-safety precaution. Because delivery trucks use the alley, the handrails did not extend all the way to the bottom of the ramp, as the ADA demands; if they did, trucks would knock them down forthwith. The ramp was also steeper than the ADA allows. Since federal ADA regulations don't require this exit ramp, the feds decided Taylor should remove it. Disgusted, Taylor says, "You can't use common sense—would you rather use a ramp slightly too steep without handrails all the way to the end, or would you rather die in a fire?" The ramp is now gone.

The suit was settled with a $16,000 fine. Six thousand dollars of it went to protesters from Atlantis/ADAPT, a local handicapped-activist group that picketed the Barolo Grill.

"The federal government flew two attorneys for every meeting, gave them hotels, rental cars, meals. They came in from D.C. seven times," says Taylor. "We figure at least $250,000 was spent to force a restaurant in Denver to comply." He says the restaurant continues to average about one wheelchair-using patron a month—the same as before the case: "Nor have we ever once had a customer's wheels touch the ramp to the upper platform.". . .

Private citizens aren't the only ones bedeviled by strict application of the ADA. The Washington (D.C.) Metropolitan Area Transit Authority has already spent almost $40 million on ADA reform, says spokeswoman Patricia Lambe. So it's not just a matter of money that made them rebel against a particular ADA requirement that they found irrelevant and completely unnecessary. "It's principle and science," Lambe insists, explaining D.C. Metro's refusal to change the platform edging in all their train stations to a raised surface of rubber bumps—allegedly to prevent blind riders from falling in front of trains.

> *"The Washington (D.C.) Metropolitan Area Transit Authority has already spent almost $40 million on ADA reform."*

The D.C. Metro system commissioned a study that found the current platform edging perfectly suitable to prevent that tragedy—which occurs far less frequently than sighted people falling. The rare falls by the blind that have occurred were caused by things other than the difference in surfacing between the edge and the main platform anyway, Lambe insists. "Where is the data saying this was ever a problem?"

Besides, she says, the ADA was meant to be a civil rights law, not a safety regulation. The D.C. Metro system told the Federal Transit Administration it intends to keep its current platform edging. Instead, under an agreement with the FTA, the Metro will intensify the flashing lights at the platform edge.

For many individuals and municipal authorities, though, cost *is* the issue. The National Association of Counties estimates the ADA will cost counties $2.8 billion to comply from 1994–98. The U.S. Conference of Mayors sees cities spending $2.2 billion over the same period.

> "The estimates of the ADA's costs are almost certainly skewed downward . . . by advocates."

Consider sidewalk curb cuts, which provide mini-ramps for wheelchair users on city sidewalks. Various municipalities estimate the cost of installing the cuts at $500 to $4,000 each—and most cities have a lot of curbs. The ADA's curb-cut requirement kicks in any time work is done on roads or sidewalks. Philadelphia lost a suit in which it argued that merely resurfacing the street in front of the sidewalk shouldn't mean having to replace the curbs. Now just filling potholes can trigger ADA-related sidewalk overhauls.

Many cities, like many businesses, are simply flouting the law. The official deadline for ADA compliance for local governments was January 26, 1995, and no one is pretending this means anyone is actually in compliance. Every town and county in the nation is a lawsuit away from serious trouble.

Faulty Estimates

Still, ADA experts at municipal government associations emphasize that good-faith efforts with the disabled community can insulate cities from suits. Governments can avoid expensive structural retrofitting by emphasizing "program compliance" instead of "structural compliance": holding meetings downstairs instead of upstairs, for instance.

John Storm and Roman Yasiejko of the Duchess County (New York) Department of Health . . . insist that municipalities *can* comply. They did, not by hiring expensive outside consultants to examine their 800,000 square feet of office space but by putting together a complicated structure of city-employee teams. In the end, Storm and Yasiejko calculate that the actual cost of bringing the county into almost 99 percent ADA compliance was only $330,000, substantially less than their first estimate of $800,000, which included money for outside consultants.

But they get this figure by assuming the labor of all the employees was absolutely costless. Yes, the project required them to form multi-level teams to examine every square inch of their office property and come up with ways to bring it up to the standards of a complex law that none of them had any previous experience with. But, says Yasiejko sincerely, those employees weren't officially relieved of any of their other duties, so the project cost nothing extra.

Duchess County also found savings by foisting compliance expenses onto the private landlords from whom they lease space. Under the law, says Yasiejko, "the private sector has less flexibility with compliance than the public. So will the county pay, or the landlord? There's a very competitive market for buyers of leased spaces, so in most cases the landlords bore the cost."

This misplaced sense of costlessness—ignoring expenses sloughed off on others, assuming no opportunity cost to lost time (or space)—often contaminates estimates of the low cost of ADA compliance. For example, a handicapped space in a small stripmall parking lot could be considered as cheap as spray-painting the silhouette of someone in a wheelchair—or as expensive as lost business when people leave because they can't find a parking space.

And sure, some modifications, like putting desks up on cinderblocks to make room for wheelchairs—an example beloved by ADA devotees—are cheap and easy. But at least in that case, the modification is in response to an actual existing problem—a real employee in a wheelchair.

Expensive Modifications

Consider a more-typical "public accommodation" modification triggered by construction work in the offices of the Reason Foundation, the nonprofit think tank that publishes *Reason*. Although the modern office building in which the foundation is located complies with most ADA requirements—from wide doors to Braille elevator buttons—most suites have conventional noisy fire alarms. So when the foundation spent $1,100 to install a couple of half-walls dividing offices, it was required to fork over another $5,000 (to a different contractor) for strobe-light fire alarms for the deaf. The foundation has no deaf employees, and the chance that a deaf visitor would be around during a fire and not have any hearing person warn them is infinitesimal. But the law is the law. And $5,000 is a lot of money.

> *"Every business, every public building, every government in the country is living under the shadow of a potentially . . . financially devastating lawsuit."*

The estimates of the ADA's costs are almost certainly skewed downward, perhaps unintentionally, by advocates. The Job Accommodation Network, a government-funded disability consulting service at West Virginia University, is often cited for its figures emphasizing the very low costs of accommodating the disabled in the workplace. Their data, based on surveys (with a 45 percent response rate) of people who call them seeking advice, indicate that 68 percent of ADA accommodations cost less than $500, and that only 22 percent cost more than $1,000. The median cost, calculates the network, is $200 per accommodation: the average, $992.

Some lawyers guess that those figures are in the ballpark. But Wendy Lechner of the National Federation of Independent Businesses calls them "complete hooey." She says, "There is no meaningful average. We know that small business owners are not being surveyed to find out their costs. It's all anecdotal evidence from a small amount of respondents.". . .

Few Positive Results

All indications are that the ADA simply cannot be obeyed in its entirety. Which means every business, every public building, every government in the country is living under the shadow of a potentially exhausting and financially devastating lawsuit.

And for what? Like research into ADA's macro costs, research into its benefits has been thin. But the data that exist are not encouraging.

> *"The ADA [has not] shown any signs of stanching the flow of federal disability relief money."*

The National Organization on Disabilities conducted a survey on the status of the disabled in America in 1986 and again in 1994. The big numbers are numbing: 49 million disabled, more than one of six people of working age (defined as between 15 and 64). Fifteen percent, this survey says, have back problems as their only disability.

The specific figures are more striking. When Congress was considering the ADA, its advocates emphasized the benefits of making the disabled taxpayers, instead of tax consumers, by giving them freer access to jobs. But the ADA has had no appreciable effect on getting the disabled into the workforce.

In fact, the percentage of working-age disabled actually working went down from the 1986 survey—31 percent were working in 1994, compared with 33 percent in 1986. A similar study done by Vocational Econometrics Inc. found that the percentage of disabled males working or actively looking for work dropped to 30 percent in 1993 from 33 percent in 1992.

Nor has the ADA shown any signs of stanching the flow of federal disability relief money. Total benefit payments from the Social Security's disability insurance trust fund were $40.4 billion for fiscal 1995, up substantially from the $30.4 billion in 1992, when the ADA went into effect.

The data don't prove the ADA has *not* had benefits in bringing the disabled into the workplace—perhaps without the ADA their employment rate would have been even lower. But there is certainly no evidence, despite all the costs, that the ADA has helped.

George Kroloff, a spokesman for the National Organization on Disabilities, still thinks the ADA has done some—unquantifiable—good: "We're seeing the disabled presented more positively in movies, advertising, TV shows. . . . The tenor of the nation, in some not-measurable way, is more caring than it has been in the past."

If that's true, then perhaps draconian legal solutions to the problem of handicapped access aren't necessary, especially since there's no indication that the

ADA approach has worked except to satisfy the activist groups that have claimed the scalps of the likes of Blair Taylor. . . .

Reforming the ADA

Clear and precise definitions of "reasonable accommodation" and "undue burden"—such as dollar caps—are a necessary first step in ADA reform. The law ought to recognize that sometimes it makes more sense to help a person in a wheelchair up a step or two than to spend thousands of dollars on ramps. It ought to realize that if someone in a wheelchair can sit and eat in a restaurant it's not necessary to force the owner to go to heroic measures to make sure that person can sit *everywhere* in the restaurant. . . .

The courts may provide some redress. Currently, as New Haven ADA lawyer Patrick Shea puts it, "The regulations don't say anything about cost-benefit analyses. You might have to spend $100,000 to accommodate someone on a job that is only worth $25,000 to you. Tough. You've been conscripted to provide opportunities."

A decision by Seventh Circuit Appeals Judge Richard Posner, in *Lori L. Vande Zande v. State of Wisconsin Department of Administration*, may be the key to ending that conscription. Posner concluded that "even if an employer is so large or wealthy . . . that it would not be able to plead 'undue hardship,' it would not be required to expend enormous sums in order to bring about a trivial improvement. . . . If the nation's employers have potentially unlimited financial obligations to [all] disabled persons, the ADA will have imposed an indirect tax potentially greater than the national debt."

Instead of requiring an open-ended obligation, wrote Posner, "The employee must show that the accommodation is reasonable in the sense both of efficacious and of proportional to costs. Even if the prima facie showing is made, the employer has an opportunity to prove that . . . the costs are excessive in relation either to the benefits of the accommodation or to the employer's financial survival or health."

> *"Sometimes it makes more sense to help a person in a wheelchair up a step or two than to spend thousands of dollars on ramps."*

That precedent could go a long way toward . . . providing a clearer understanding of what the employment aspect of the law requires. (It could be applied to access issues as well.) It is a good first step, and it has the ADA activist community worried.

Sitting in the handicapped-accessible restaurant that cost him more months and more thousands of dollars and more grief than he could have imagined, Blair Taylor says, "I want to be helpful because I'm a nice person. I don't want to be forced to do something to help you to the detriment of my own well-being."

The ADA Defines Disability Too Broadly

by James Bovard

About the author: *James Bovard is the author of* Lost Rights: The Destruction of American Liberty *and* Shakedown: How Government Screws You from A to Z.

Federal disability policy is rapidly becoming the Bush administration's legacy to nightclub comics. But few laws in recent memory have sown as much uncertainty and legal chaos as the Americans with Disabilities Act (ADA), passed at President George Bush's urging in 1990. The act defined disability as "(a) a physical or mental impairment that substantially limits one or more of the major life activities of such individual; (b) a record of such an impairment; or (c) being regarded as having such an impairment."

A Wide Definition

Julie C. Janofsky, an attorney who has written about the ADA for the *Wall Street Journal*, notes that the definition "casts so wide a net that it includes even allergies and learning problems. And because disabilities are self-identified by the employee under the ADA, that means that the accommodations required of the employer are also defined by the employee. Once an employee identifies himself or herself as having a 'disability,' there are virtually no limits to what accommodations can be demanded."

A combination of good intentions, vague standards, and coercion, the ADA is a growing fiasco for both the private sector and local governments. This legislation has turned disabilities into valuable legal assets, prizes to be cultivated and flourished in courtrooms for financial windfalls.

In November 1994, four years after Congress passed the act—and long after the Justice Department and the Equal Employment Opportunity Commission (EEOC) had begun filing a barrage of lawsuits against private companies— EEOC chairman Gilbert Casellas admitted that his agency had yet to issue guidelines on what constitutes a disability. (The EEOC issued expansive new "guidelines" on the definition of disability in March 1995, but these only added to the pervasive uncertainty as to what the law means.) . . .

Preposterous Claims

Almost any condition can be grounds for a lawsuit in the absence of meaningful guidelines, and the ADA has already opened up a Pandora's box of lunatic claims and federal rulings. Preposterous precedents are being established; cases are being heard that should be dismissed out of hand. Some of the most egregious examples include the following:

• The EEOC announced in August 1993 that obesity was a "protected" disability under the ADA, and successfully intervened in the case of a 300-pound woman who wanted to be a nurse's aide in Rhode Island; the hospital had claimed that she would be incapable of performing essential functions of the job. The fact that a person's weight usually results from voluntary behavior did not curb the EEOC's zeal. The agency ruled that "Voluntariness is irrelevant when determining whether a condition constitutes an impairment."

• Dwayne "Fishbone" Richardson, a 410-pound Bronx subway cleaner, sued the New York Transit Authority for refusing to promote him to train operator. The Transit Authority stated that an operator, among other duties, has to be able to climb under a stalled train to make minor adjustments—something Mr. Richardson's 60-inch waistline made impossible.

• The Los Angeles Disabled Access Appeals Commission invoked the ADA in 1994 to force the Odd Ball Cabaret, a nude strip joint, to close a shower stall on its stage. The commission ruled that since the shower stall would not be accessible to a stripper in a wheelchair, the business discriminated against handicapped women. City disability official Ron Shigeta complained to the *Los Angeles Times*, "It's unfair for the media to have exploited the shower dispute to its own ends, while ignoring the important work of the Disabled Access Appeals Commission."

> *"Few laws . . . have sown as much uncertainty and legal chaos as the Americans with Disabilities Act."*

• In Santa Monica, California, a deaf woman sued Burger King, claiming that its drive-through windows illegally discriminated against deaf people. Burger King settled the lawsuit by agreeing to install visual electronic ordering devices at ten restaurants.

• Thomas Burns, a guidance counselor at Stafford High School in Hartford, Connecticut, sued under the ADA after he was fired following his arrest for cocaine possession. The *Hartford Courant* reported that Burns's lawyer said that since Burns's cocaine dependence was a disability, the school had discriminated against him.

• Ayreh Motzkin, a 60-year-old philosophy professor, is suing Boston University after being fired for allegedly sexually assaulting a female professor and sexually harassing three students. A university committee also concluded that Motzkin had violated school policy by providing alcohol to undergraduate students. Motzkin denies the charges, yet claims that tranquilizers and anti-depressants he was taking "loosened his inhibitions" and led to the alleged sexual transgressions. Claiming that he is mentally handicapped, Motzkin in his suit charges the university with violating the ADA. As the *Boston Globe* reported, "Once students complained about his behavior, Motzkin alleges, the university was aware of his handicap and had an obligation to help him deal with it."

Fashionable "Disabilities"

Just as bad as the elevation of social pathologies to civil rights is the proliferation of new "disabilities," among which "multiple chemical sensitivity"—to perfumes, aftershaves, and the like—is becoming one of the most fashionable:

• Congress appropriated a quarter-million dollars to examine Multiple Chemical Sensitivity, and scores of lawsuits alleging discrimination against MCS sufferers have been filed. Paul Imperiale, disability coordinator for the mayor's office in San Francisco, predicted in January 1995: "Ten years from now it will be politically incorrect to wear perfumes in public."

• In San Mateo, California, Beatrice Shaw sued Citicorp Credit Services for firing her because of her severe body odor. Co-workers reportedly got sick just from being near her; one of her bosses swore he could smell her from 35 feet away. A jury rejected Shaw's claim that her odor was a handicap that her employer was obliged to tolerate, but the suit cost Citicorp Credit tens of thousands of dollars in legal costs.

• In April 1995, a Madison, Wisconsin, telephone operator sued her employer for refusing to make reasonable accommodations for her narcolepsy. The woman was routinely late for work, and had sought permission to continue arriving late owing to her "disability." Many similar suits have also been filed.

The ADA is also exploding like a series of cluster bombs across the budgets of local governments across the country:

"Once an employee identifies himself or herself as having a 'disability,' there are virtually no limits to what accommodations can be demanded."

• The National Association of Counties estimates that county governments will be forced to spend almost $3 billion by 1998 to comply with ADA mandates.

• On May 1, 1995, the village board of Silver Creek, New York, voted to more than double a proposed tax-rate hike to finance compliance with the ADA.

• The Webster Elementary School in Magna, Utah—a landmark in the small community for nearly a century—may be closed down because of the ADA. The local ADA compliance committee said in May 1995 that it could cost $1 million to bring the school up to ADA standards.

• San Francisco's Bay Area Rapid Transit raised fares 15 percent in April 1995, in part to pay for modifications mandated by the ADA.

• Anti-smokers are invoking the ADA to compel governments to ban smoking in restaurants. A federal appeals court in Boston ruled in April 1995 that three asthmatic children and one adult with lupus could sue McDonald's and Burger King for not "accommodating" them by prohibiting smoking. A panel of judges ruled that the plaintiffs' allegations that "the restaurants they visited contained too much smoke to allow their equal use of the facilities . . . might support a blanket ban" of smoking. (An ADA lawsuit against a Texas nightclub that allowed smoking was thrown out of court in January 1995.)

> *"The EEOC [Equal Employment Opportunity Commission] announced . . . that obesity was a 'protected' disability under the ADA."*

• In March 1993, a federal judge ruled that the District of Columbia's practice of excluding blind people from jury service was a violation of the ADA.

Accommodating Violent Employees

One consequence of the ADA has been to weaken employers' ability to prevent violence in the workplace. David Fram, an ADA policy attorney with EEOC, warned in a speech in 1994 that discipline standards for employees who attack their bosses must not conflict with the company's duty to reasonably accommodate the mentally disabled. (I called Fram and asked for a copy of the speech. He told me that he hadn't been speaking from a text, and that even if he had been, the speech was confidential—even though it was summarized in the *Bureau of National Affairs Daily Business Report*.)

The *Employee Relations Law Journal* noted, "Many individuals who become violent toward customers or coworkers suffer from some form of mental disorder. Yet for an employer to be too careful in screening potentially dangerous persons out of the work force is to invite liability for discrimination under the ADA, while to be not careful enough is to invite tragedy and horrendous liability for negligent hire or negligent retention." Such conflicts have already made their way into court:

• In Maine, Thomas Lussier, a Postal Service employee who suffers from "post-traumatic stress disorder," was fired after his supervisors became convinced that his agitated behavior, panic attacks, and "volatile personality" could lead him to go on a shooting spree. (Shortly beforehand, two postal employees had gone on shooting sprees elsewhere.) A federal judge found that the firing violated the ADA because of its "unwarranted generalizations drawn from beliefs about Lussier's handicap." The judge noted: "The Postal Service could have fired Lussier for his irascibility alone," but that once his "handicap" was a factor, the firing became illegal.

• In Tampa, Florida, Joe Hindman was fired from GTE Data Services after he was found to have robbed purses in the office of thousands of dollars and was caught bringing a loaded gun into the office. Hindman sued the company, claiming he was disabled because of a chemical imbalance caused by the prescription drug Prozac. Federal judge Elizabeth Kovachevich ruled that the company violated the man's civil rights, saying, "When poor judgment is a symptom of a mental or psychological disorder, it is defined as an impairment that would qualify as a disability under the ADA." To allow Hindman to continue working at the company, Kovachevich ruled, the company should have tried to find some "reasonable accommodation." Kovachevich's decision was later overturned.

Work Hazards

The ADA discrimination rules pose other threats to nondisabled workers. *Crain's Chicago Business* reported the following case in 1994:

> A factory crane operator was diagnosed with bipolar personality disorder (also known as manic depression). He took lithium to control it, and had never exhibited any aberrant behavior on the job. Still, co-workers feared that a manic episode would occur while he was operating the crane, resulting in serious injury to others. . . . However, in this case, the crane operator was protected by the ADA because of his excellent track record on lithium.

A crane operator who forgets to take his medicine can do far more damage with a 500-pound wrecking ball than a listless government file clerk with the same condition who makes the same mistake.

> *"One consequence of the ADA has been to weaken employers' ability to prevent violence in the workplace."*

Claims of discrimination based on mental disability are one of the most frequent charges under the ADA. The EEOC defined mental disability as simply a "mental impairment," which was equated with "mental disorder." Since the EEOC's definition is so vague, the official definitions of mental illness of the American Psychiatric Association for mental illnesses are often relied on for court cases. Yet these definitions are also very expansive. The psychiatric association recently defined "disorder of written expression" (i.e., bad writing) and excessive use of caffeine as potential illnesses.

The *Employee Relations Law Journal* noted in 1995 that the ADA may be found to "protect" personality disorders such as:

• Antisocial Personality Disorder—a pattern of disregard for, and violation of the rights of, others.
• Histrionic Personality Disorder—a pattern of excessive emotionality and attention seeking.
• Narcissistic Personality Disorder—a pattern of grandiosity, need for admira-

tion, and lack of empathy. Psychiatrist John Fielder complained in 1994, "The ADA reads as if employee requests for accommodation should be accepted at face value, when this should never be the case."

Learning "Disabilities"

At colleges, the ADA has been a godsend to shirking students. Thousands have successfully dodged required courses by getting a shrink to certify them as "math-disabled." The *Palm Beach Post* noted in December 1994, "Even though the ADA made little change in the services that [colleges] were required to offer students, the publicity given the law made many more students and their parents aware of the opportunity to qualify as disabled." The ADA has also left many colleges unable to discipline or discharge disruptive students. Victoria McGillian, dean of Wheaton College, told the *Boston Globe* that, because of the ADA, "students who fit the admissions criteria but who might not have been actively considered are now being accepted if they are otherwise qualified. We cannot rule out a psychotic student if otherwise capable."

> *"Claims of discrimination based on mental disability are one of the most frequent charges under the ADA."*

Jon Westling, president of Boston University, commented in May 1995 that ADA lawsuits and threats have resulted in demands "to keep learning disabled philosophy students safe from the perplexities of Aristotle, to accommodate foreign-language majors who have foreign-language phobia, and to comfort physics students who suffer from dyscalculia, which is, of course, the particular learning disablement that prevents one from learning math." One Tufts University student invoked the ADA to claim that the university was obliged to "accommodate" her aversion to taking tests.

The ADA is sometimes said to stand for "Attorneys' Dreams Answered." Even when ludicrous ADA cases are thrown out of courts, they can chill the legal atmosphere for employers. When the Civil Rights Act was passed in 1964, it was assumed that only cases of clear racial bias would be applicable under the law. However, successive waves of foolish court decisions and EEOC power grabs have transformed employment law into a caricature of Congress's intent. As a result, businesses routinely settle even completely baseless discrimination charges out of court, because the average cost of defending a case is roughly $80,000. The same pattern of lavish payoffs for bogus charges appears to be repeating itself with the ADA.

• A group of aging stewardesses sued Delta Airlines over its weight guidelines for employees, but did not explain how heavier stews could finesse their way around a drinks cart in the minuscule aisle of a Boeing 727.

• A 360-pound woman sued a Memphis movie theater, claiming that she deserved $1.5 million for her emotional distress when it turned out that none of the theater seats was large enough to accommodate her.

• A Suffolk University professor sued the law school, claiming that she had been denied tenure because she suffered from an illness that results in lethargy and decreased productivity.

• A clerk-typist in the Howard County, Maryland government was fired after repeatedly directing rude outbursts and denunciations at her supervisors. She claimed in her suit that the firing violated her civil rights. Because she is a manic depressive, she claimed that her employer was required to strip her job of all its inherent stress.

More Frivolous Lawsuits

• A motorist who was ticketed by a Topeka, Kansas, policeman for not wearing a seatbelt claimed that he could not wear one because of claustrophobia, and sued the city for violating the ADA. A judge dismissed the suit in December 1993.

• A New Orleans television broadcaster, Lynn Gansar, received an EEOC endorsement to sue her employer for refusing to give her extensive time off to try to get pregnant. This put the station—"because of her pregnancy-related condition," the agency wrote—in violation of the ADA. In April, a jury rejected her demands for back pay and severance pay.

• A man who had repeatedly been hospitalized for heart failure, and who had a serious risk of losing consciousness from his uncontrolled diabetes, invoked the ADA to sue Frederick County, Maryland, for refusing to retain him as a bus driver. (He was discharged after failing federal and state health examinations required for commercial bus drivers.) A federal appeals court spiked the suit on March 29, 1995, concluding that the driver would be a risk to himself, his passengers, pedestrians, and other motorists.

> *"At colleges, the ADA has been a godsend to shirking students."*

• Donald Winston, an English instructor at Central Maine Technical College, was fired after he invited a female student to a private meeting, talked about sex, and then kissed her. She filed sexual harassment charges, and Winston acknowledged having sex with other female students (one other student complained of sexual harassment). Winston sued the college, claiming that his firing constituted discrimination against the handicapped. Two doctors testified at his trial that he suffered from a "sexual addiction."

• A federal judge rejected the suit of a postal worker who had destroyed property and endangered his supervisor, and then claimed to be suffering from "explosive personality disorder."

• Florida district appeals judge Eugene Garrett was nabbed shoplifting a VCR remote control; when the Florida Supreme Court ordered Garrett removed from the bench, Garrett appealed the removal, citing the ADA. Garrett claimed he was disabled because he was "depressed" because his daughter failed to get into law school and his son was getting poor grades in school.

• A former FBI communications officer was fired after his supervisors concluded that his paranoia and inability to perceive reality interfered with his ability to handle confidential documents. A federal judge noted that the employee "at one point felt he had died and gone to hell. He feared that a nuclear holocaust was imminent, and he called the Strategic Air Command in Omaha to issue a warning." The FBI employee sued, claiming discrimination against his "bipolar mood disorder."

Better Ways to Help the Disabled

In the face of such frivolous suits, some judges are beginning to lose patience. On March 8, 1995, federal judge Samuel Kent denounced an ADA suit as "a blatant attempt to extort money," after a man who, eight days earlier, had been awarded damages for permanent disability status from the Santa Fe Railroad, sued the railroad for refusing to rehire him because of his disability. The judge condemned the suit as "either blatantly fraudulent or utterly ridiculous."

Despite the ADA's blunt threats to force employers to hire more handicapped people, the percentage of disabled who have jobs is actually lower now than before the law was enacted in 1990. If disabled people take a job, they lose their federal Medicare coverage as well as Supplemental Security Income payments. As a result, many disabled have chosen not to accept work even when they could find it. They are in the same "trap" as welfare mothers—unable to take a low- or mid-level job without risking a real decline in their income. Gary Edwards of United Cerebral Palsy of Birmingham, Alabama, told the *New York Times* in October 1994, "We have built up a system . . . that says it is not in your best interest to go to work."

Society can and should help those who cannot help themselves. If people want to provide more help to the handicapped, it would be far more effective to provide additional subsidies to employers to hire the disabled—as is currently being done under numerous federal and state programs. But it is dishonest for the government to endow some people with the legal power to make unlimited demands from others through litigation and claim that the result is simply "equal opportunity."

In March 1995, the EEOC issued a ruling expanding the definition of disability to include an inability to perform functions such as "thinking, concentrating, and interacting with other people." Under this definition, who knows how many people in Washington alone might qualify.

Chapter 2

How Should Society Help the Disabled?

Chapter Preface

During a dispute in the early hours of July 24, 1988, Armando Dimas was shot in the neck. The bullet lodged high in his spinal cord, paralyzing him from the jaw down. From that day on, Dimas would be unable to breathe without a ventilator, unable to move his arms or legs, unable to feed or dress himself. The doctors who first treated Dimas at the emergency room at Hermann Hospital in Houston, Texas, were surprised that he lived through the night.

When it became apparent that Dimas would indeed survive, the question became what to do with him. Dimas, his parents, and his eleven siblings were illegal immigrants from Mexico. His parents felt that they did not have the resources or the expertise to care for their quadriplegic son at home. The ventilator in particular intimidated Dimas's family. "We aren't educated enough to run that machine," his mother worried. "Something will happen to him, and we won't know what to do." However, Dimas and his family also could not afford to pay his rapidly rising hospital bill, which reached $57,000 in only three weeks. With the hospital already strapped for funds, the financial directors knew that they would not be able to foot Dimas's bill forever.

For a while, a compromise solution appeared to be working. On November 1, 1988, Dimas was transferred to the Total Life Care Center, a residential facility designed for severely disabled patients. Hermann Hospital still paid his medical bill, but the cost of his care was greatly reduced. In addition, Dimas enjoyed living at the center more than the hospital. He went on trips to the mall and to ball games with other residents, and his family visited every weekend.

Within four years, though, Dimas's care at the Total Life Care Center had increased to $12,000 a month. The hospital decided that it could no longer afford to pay Dimas's bills and determined that he would be sent home on October 31, 1992. His apprehensive family was given a month to learn how to handle the machines whose functionings are essential to his survival. At first, Dimas was angry. "Why don't they just wheel me out to the sidewalk and let me die?" he asked. But as his family members gained confidence about their ability to care for him, Dimas became less frightened and more content to be at home.

Like Dimas, many people with disabilities require expensive equipment, medical treatments, or daily assistance that they and their families cannot afford or perform on their own. The following chapter examines debates over the extent to which society should help these disabled individuals.

Welfare Programs for the Disabled Should Be Reformed

by Carolyn L. Weaver

About the author: *Carolyn L. Weaver is the director of Social Security and Pension Studies at the American Enterprise Institute, a public policy research organization. She is the author of* Disability and Work.

President Bill Clinton claims his welfare reform plan will "end welfare as we know it." Yet his plan fails to tackle the federal government's largest and fastest-growing cash welfare program, Supplemental Security Income (SSI)—now more costly and growing much more rapidly than AFDC (Aid to Families with Dependent Children), the focus of the welfare reform debate. Established to serve the elderly and people with disabilities, SSI's poor targeting of benefits has caused the program to double in cost between 1980 and 1994. Ironically, at the same time the federal government is trying to expand work opportunities for the disabled under the Americans with Disabilities Act, SSI is encouraging growing numbers of disabled Americans to live a life of dependency on government.

A Growing Problem

In 1993, an estimated 6 million people received Supplemental Security Income, up nearly one-half since 1980 and one-quarter just since 1990. Federal spending on SSI stood at $23 billion, double its level (in real dollars) in 1980. By contrast, federal spending on AFDC, the government's best-known welfare program, totaled $16 billion in 1993, up 23 percent in real terms since 1980. According to the fiscal year 1995 Clinton budget, SSI benefits are growing so rapidly that, by the end of the 1990s, the cost of the program (including federal and state spending) will exceed the cost of AFDC, food stamps, subsidized housing, the greatly expanded Earned Income Tax Credit, and every other major welfare program except Medicaid.

Excerpted from Carolyn L. Weaver, "Welfare Payments to the Disabled," *American Enterprise*, January/February 1995. Reprinted by permission of the *American Enterprise*, a Washington-based magazine of politics, business, and culture.

SSI's expansion spells increased pressure on both Medicaid, the nation's giant health care program for the poor, and food stamps, since SSI recipients qualify for both of these programs. In the case of Medicaid, the cost of health care for the aged and disabled poor is much higher than average. According to the House Ways and Means Committee, in 1992, Medicaid spending averaged $2,936 per person—but was $7,700 for the elderly and $7,612 for people with disabilities, compared with $1,752 for AFDC adults and $959 for AFDC children. The bulk (approximately 70 percent) of Medicaid spending is for the aged and disabled, not AFDC mothers and children as often assumed.

> *"Young people with mental disorders are the fastest growing segment of the adult [Supplemental Security Income] population."*

Traditionally, SSI has enjoyed unusual support on Capitol Hill and remarkable protection at budget time. In contrast to AFDC, SSI provides a guaranteed minimum income ($5,496 annually for individuals and $8,244 for couples) that is increased annually with the cost of living and is financed almost entirely by the federal government. Most serious discussion of SSI reform—or Social Security reform for that matter—has brought forth proposals for expanding eligibility and increasing payment levels. The recommendations of a 1992 study panel on SSI, convened by the commissioner of Social Security, had a five-year price tag of $100 billion! . . .

SSI's seeming immunity from reform stems partially from an outdated view that the program primarily functions as a safety net for the elderly poor. While once true, SSI has been transformed over the years into a program serving mainly working-age adults (and increasingly children) with disabilities.

When SSI was created in 1974—federalizing old-age assistance, aid to the disabled, and aid to the blind programs around the country—most SSI recipients *were* elderly people, generally those who were not eligible for Social Security or whose pensions left them in poverty. Over the years, as the incomes of the elderly have risen, the number of elderly people receiving SSI has fallen. (Elderly immigrants, who now make up 28 percent of the elderly rolls—up from 5 percent in 1982—are an exception, and the growth in their relative numbers prompted legislation in 1993 to tighten family support requirements.) At the same time—for reasons that are not entirely clear—the number of disabled recipients has soared, doubling between 1974 and 1990 and increasing by over 1 million between 1991 and 1994 alone.

The Typical Recipient

What do we know about SSI-disability recipients? The typical recipient is in his or her thirties or forties, has a high school education or less, and was granted benefits on the basis of a mental disorder, such as schizophrenia, depression, or anxiety. Fully 57 percent of adults on SSI-disability have a mental disorder. Young people with mental disorders are the fastest growing segment of the adult SSI population. The prospects that these people will ever return to work (or go to work) are very poor.

Thanks to a 1990 court order and new regulations that loosened eligibility for children, children with disabilities are the fastest growing segment of the SSI population today. Stretching SSI in ways never contemplated in 1974, 225,000 children with disabilities (mainly mental disorders, including the much-discussed attention deficit disorder, and mental retardation) were added to the rolls in 1993, triple the number in 1989. The number of children on the rolls now approaches 1 million, or close to one out of five people on the SSI-disability rolls.

Tens of thousands of alcoholics and drug addicts have also found their way onto the SSI rolls, and their ranks are growing rapidly. According to the Social Security Administration, the number of people on the rolls with substance abuse as their primary disorder (in other words, without some other qualifying disability, such as cancer or heart disease) nearly quadrupled in the three-and-a-half-year period October 1990 to April 1994, rising from 23,000 to 86,000. The General Accounting Office reports that between the two disability programs administered by the Social Security Administration—SSI-disability and Disability Insurance (which, like the Social Security retirement program, pays benefits to covered workers based on their average earnings while working, not based on financial need)—250,000 drug addicts and alcoholics are receiving monthly benefits at an annual cost of $1.4 billion, with over half of these addicts added to the rolls between 1989 and 1994. . . .

Cutting Back on Dependency

Encouraging and enabling people to overcome their disabilities to work and targeting assistance on those who can actually benefit from it should be essential ingredients of SSI reform.

At the point of entry to the program, SSI creates strong disincentives to work, disincentives that are no less potent than in AFDC. Once on the benefit rolls, SSI recipients receive cash assistance, but no rehabilitation, job training, or employment services—services that are no less necessary to enable people with disabilities to find work than they are for single parents receiving AFDC. And in providing cash support with few strings attached, SSI tends to perpetuate the very conditions that preclude work and promote dependency.

> *"250,000 drug addicts and alcoholics are receiving monthly [disability] benefits at an annual cost of $1.4 billion."*

Further, SSI poses problems of eligibility that dwarf those in AFDC. Whether in assessing an adult's ability to engage in "substantial gainful activity" or a child's ability to engage in "age-appropriate activities of daily living," the government's decisions about who is disabled and to what extent are costly, complex, inherently subjective, and frequently disputed. This raises many questions about the design of SSI, not the least of which is whether it should even cover disabled children eligible for AFDC and Medicaid—which, in turn, raises a question as to how much more the families of these children should receive for basic support than the families of other poor children. . . .

Outdated Assumptions

For adults, the Social Security disability programs are premised on an outdated assumption that people with disabilities cannot, and very likely never will be able to, work. The "once disabled always disabled" assumption of the 1950s and 1960s remains deeply embedded in current policy, despite dramatic improvements in science and medicine, in technology and information, and in the educational opportunities of young people with disabilities. These advances have improved the quality of life of people with disabilities—who are also now protected from job discrimination by the strict mandates of the Americans with Disabilities Act—and have created new opportunities for work. Yet the number of people on the Social Security disability rolls has never been higher. In 1993, some 9 million people (including family members) received checks from the Social Security Administration totaling $59 billion. Most disability recipients are prime-age men and women who will never leave the benefit rolls.

In a 1992 Syracuse University study, Leo Aarts, Richard V. Burkhauser, and Philip de Jong carefully reviewed disability policies in the United States, Sweden (where 14 percent of workers were "disabled" in 1989), the Netherlands, and Germany. They concluded that "the root cause of the increasing incidence of disability over the past two decades has more to do with policy medicine" administered to "health-impaired workers than with any change in the underlying health of citizens."

If the nation is agreed that neither disabilities nor welfare benefits should prevent citizens from working, then ending "welfare as we know it" must include an overhaul of the federal disability programs.

Welfare Programs for the Disabled Should Not Be Cut

by Marta Russell

About the author: *Marta Russell is a disabilities activist and freelance writer based in Los Angeles, California.*

The new congressional lingo—welfare "transformation" and "personal responsibility"—is Orwellian Newtspeak for people with disabilities, masking the reality of what the Contract With America [legislation proposed by the Republican-controlled Congress] actually portends for us. House Speaker Newt Gingrich claims that the Republican "devolution" plan will empower state governments to become more efficient. But isn't this an expedient ideology, when the details are missing as to how states will accomplish this "efficiency" and succeed where the federal government has failed? For disabled people, the devil will be in the details. How will the states handle their new mandate?

Drastic Cuts

If enacted, the Republican plan, including the Personal Responsibility Act of 1995, would drastically decrease the Supplemental Security Income (SSI) program for children, end children's entitlement to SSI, lump twenty to thirty welfare programs together, and cap the total federal expenditure on them so that programs will no longer increase to meet public need. [The Personal Responsibility Act (HR 4) was vetoed by President Bill Clinton on January 9, 1996.] Since the states will be given free rein to spend as they please with no requirement to continue existing programs, disability along with other programs face reduction or extinction.

The House has targeted Medicaid for drastic spending cuts. If the program is block-granted, the states will get 75 percent of the Medicaid money they currently receive, and they would be allowed to disburse these reduced funds with

Excerpted from Marta Russell, "A Contract on the Disabled: How Republican Plans Threaten People with Disabilities," *Democratic Left*, July/August 1995. Reprinted with permission.

few, if any, strings attached. Because people with disabilities and those over 65 years old account for 27 percent of Medicaid recipients but use 67 percent of the funds, disabled persons will be disproportionately affected by these cuts.

For people who need the support of these programs, "devolution" becomes a code word for de-funding. If the Republican block-grant plan succeeds, 27 percent of the roughly 900,000 children in the SSI program will be denied benefits. By shaving off 20 percent of the money allocated to these federal programs and distributing only 80 percent to the states, Republicans project a total savings of $69.4 billion. The House budget cuts $189 billion out of Medicaid funds.

> *"Many [Supplemental Security Income] recipients could be forced into the streets because they will not be able both to pay rent and buy food."*

Since block-granting allows the states to decide how to divvy up the capped funds among many competing programs, disabled persons living on SSI ($400–600 per month) could lose their access to "Section 8" housing. . . . People on SSI are not allowed food stamps. Many SSI recipients could be forced into the streets because they will not be able both to pay rent and buy food. Programs that provide for home care attendants in some states may be reduced or entirely eliminated, sending many more people into costly institutions. Disabled children will no longer be entitled to benefits. Since there will be no uniformity in delivery of services, and the entitlement to Medicaid will end, states could opt to discontinue certain Medicaid services, and more disabled people would be denied treatment.

The States' Poor Record

It can be argued that if the states could be trusted to do what is right, then social justice issues never would have had to go to the federal level in the first place. The Civil Rights Act of 1964 was implemented by the federal government because the states were not interested in eliminating discrimination against African Americans. The Family Assistance Act of 1972, which established SSI, was enacted because many poor elderly, blind, and disabled people were going hungry and homeless. One reason the Americans With Disabilities Act (ADA) of 1990 became law was because states had not complied with the access laws already established 20 years earlier by the Rehabilitation Act of 1973. . . .

It is doublethink to believe that the Republican plan to shift disability programs to the states is a genuine attempt at better government. This rhetoric is a smokescreen meant to conceal the real agenda—the undoing of government—a way to make billions of drastic program slashes in welfare and health care programs with little concern for their real impact on people.

There is outright danger in turning disability programs over to the states.

Many federal protections now exist in Medicaid law. Because state governments have a bad track record of following these mandates, consumer protection agencies have been compelled to sue them to force them to fulfill their obligations. These lawsuits are over such basic issues as the right to a fair hearing, the right to access to services, the right to due process (which includes notice if a service is to be curtailed), uniformity of standard of services, and non-discrimination in the provision of services. If Medicaid is block-granted, none of these protections will continue to exist.

With no national standard, the effects from block-granting could vary widely from state to state. States that provide exemplary services may find themselves penalized for doing the right thing. For instance, if one state were to provide decent health care coverage with all the options available, and most others provide nominal care, people could choose to move to the state that would provide the best care for them. But if this state became overrun with people needing assistance, its taxpaying citizens most likely would vote to lower their state standards to resist the migration. This dynamic will lead all states toward a lowest common denominator.

Slashing Social Services

We already have harbingers of how the states will translate the call for "reform." A trend has developed—what has been called "the race to the bottom" on social service spending. Twenty-six states have initiated welfare reform plans, often making Draconian cuts in social service programs. And the movement is spreading: California Governor Pete Wilson . . . has targeted welfare programs for slashing as a means to balance his budget. He proposes to eliminate Medicaid "optional" services, which include medical supplies, physical therapy, occupational therapy, foot care, and dental services, to further reduce costs. Wilson had made cuts to SSI two years in a row and in 1995 proposed to reduce benefits another 11.5 percent to 13 percent. This would mean a reduction of $71 per month for individuals and $149 for couples, in effect reducing grants well below the poverty level.

Federal "maintenance of effort" law makes it illegal for states to go below 1983 SSI supplement levels. But the Republicans are relentless in their desire to cut: at the request of

> *"There is outright danger in turning disability programs over to the states."*

Governor Wilson, Representative Wally Herger (R-CA) included a provision in the Personal Responsibility Act that would remove that protection. This act has passed the House. If it goes through the Senate and Clinton signs it, then California will be able to go ahead with Wilson's proposed reductions.

Many disabled Californians are adamant that if this cut forces them out of their homes, they will not go back to the institutions. They would rather risk living or dying on the streets. It costs the federal government much more to put someone in an institution than to meagerly support them in their own home.

The Gingrich solution for children on Aid to Families with Dependent Children (AFDC) is to send them to orphanages. The nursing home is the disabled's equivalent to the orphanage. If Gingrich is willing to go backwards in time to put kids into orphanages, he will be willing to "devolve" disabled people back into institutions, undoing much of what our thirty-year-old independent living movement has accomplished. Republican "transformation" then really means less freedom.

Maybe the Republicans think charity will pick up the pieces. But this is wishful thinking. Charities have admitted that they are overloaded. For disabled people, the thought of having to rely on charities is anathema. We have been working for thirty years to move away from the charity model to a civil rights model, so that disabled persons may enjoy the same *rights* other citizens enjoy. It is ironic that after passage of the ADA, those rights will be out of reach for disabled Americans who cannot withstand the fallout from cuts in welfare programs.

To this Gingrich might say: get a job, go to work. But the 60 percent of disabled people who would like to become employed have had little success with being offered jobs. We have a general unemployment rate of 70 percent. For significantly disabled persons it is 85 percent—and both of these figures are *higher* than before passage of the ADA. Congress's failure to enact disability-sensitive health care reform and to remove work disincentives from social security policies has further complicated employment for us. "Personal responsibility" then takes on a new dimension when applied to disabled people—lifting oneself up by nonexistent bootstraps is indeed Orwellian.

The Republicans surely have birthed a contract on the disabled.

Home Care Should Be Available for the Disabled

by Ruth Conniff

About the author: *Ruth Conniff is the managing editor of the* Progressive, *a liberal monthly periodical.*

On New Year's Day, 1996, hundreds of disabled people in Wisconsin suddenly confronted the prospect of entering nursing homes. The state budget, passed in fall 1995, placed a cap on funding for community-based services, including personal-attendant care. On January 1, the state began enforcing the cap. Anyone whose home care costs more than the cap was directed to the nearest residential-care facility. This has caused a wave of fear and outrage among the disabled.

Capping Medicaid

"I was in a nursing home once, and believe me, I don't ever want to be in one again," says Steve Verridan, who suffered a spinal-cord injury in a diving accident. He now works at Access to Independence, a nonprofit agency in Madison, Wisconsin, helping other disabled people find home care. When the law went into effect, Verridan—like many of his clients—had to call ten nursing homes within a fifty-mile radius of his home in order to prove they wouldn't take him. Unless his phone calls earn him an exemption, he could find himself back in an institution. "Of course you're calling these places hoping like hell to be turned down," he says.

What's happening in Wisconsin marks a dramatic shift in the way the federal and state governments treat Medicaid, the program that provides health care to millions of poor, elderly, and disabled Americans. Republicans in Congress have proposed cutting federal Medicaid funds by as much as 30 percent by 2003. And politicians of both parties—from President Bill Clinton to Wisconsin Governor Tommy Thompson, who is the head of the National Governors' Association—are advocating giving the states more flexibility to try cost-saving experiments.

"Taxpayers can no longer afford open-ended Medicaid entitlements," a memo from Wisconsin's Department of Health and Social Services explains. "For the first time in recent history, Medicaid recipients must make the same choices about care setting as private-pay individuals."

Praying for Rejection

Thus, people with disabilities in Wisconsin have become the most reluctant of shoppers, making their phone calls to nursing homes, and praying for rejection.

"We've gotten several calls . . . I've mostly talked to people in their twenties or thirties who are going to school and have jobs," says Maureen Griffin, the admissions coordinator for City View nursing home in Madison. "It's hard. I'd hate to see anyone go somewhere they don't want to be, and it seems like most of them don't want to be here. They're just looking for a 'no' answer."

Unfortunately, she says, she can't always tell her nervous callers what they want to hear.

"In some scenarios, we'd be able to meet their needs. Most often I've been saying yes, and then they try to get off the phone in a hurry. . . . There's been a couple of people I've been able to say no to because they needed transportation provided, or they had space needs, they had a pet, something like that."

According to the state, sympathetic nursing-home staff have been handing out excuses too readily.

"The state has sent out notices saying these reasons aren't good enough," says Ray Froemming of the Wisconsin Coalition for Advocacy, which is filing a lawsuit against the home-care cap. "But there was never any explanation of how people should know if what the nursing homes say is accurate. Obviously, they needed to think this through more carefully before. They're learning as they go."

> *"I was in a nursing home once, and believe me, I don't ever want to be in one again."*

Under the law, 278 people in Wisconsin are affected by the cap on the state's Community Options Program, which was created to fund community-based alternatives to nursing-home care. Another 500 to 600 people are affected by the cap on Medicaid reimbursements for home health care, the state estimates.

All of these people have home health-care expenses that exceed $2,325 per month—the average Medicaid portion of nursing-home care. The caps don't include people under twenty-two years of age or the ventilator-dependent, who are automatically exempt. People for whom no nursing-home bed is available are also exempt—if they can demonstrate that the ten nursing homes nearest them won't let them in.

Problems with Compliance

As the disabled scramble for exemptions, confusion and hard feelings abound.

"We've done what we can to comply," says Martha Desjardin of Sun Prairie,

Wisconsin, whose thirty-six-year-old daughter, Terri, has a progressive neuro-muscular disorder. Terri can't speak or get around the house without assistance. Martha, who is sixty-two and has arthritis, and her husband, who is sixty-five and has a bad back, rely on attendants to help Terri bathe and dress and get in and out of bed.

To bring Terri into compliance with the cap, the state cut back the Desjardins' attendant care to six-and-a-half hours a day. "It's just very difficult for us to handle her all by ourselves," Martha says.

Like Verridan, the Desjardins phoned ten nursing homes to try to get an exemption from the cap. "We got no's from ten places. Her skill level was too high for them to take care of her. Terri's needs are more skilled than what's available in a nursing home."

> *"Some people are terrified because they've been in nursing homes and they have not done well."*

But the state worker who handled the Desjardins' exemption told them that some of the reasons the nursing homes gave for rejecting Terri were not acceptable. So the Desjardins only got a temporary exemption. They had their full-time home health care restored, for two months. In a few weeks, they would have to start making phone calls again.

The Department of Health and Social Services points out in a memo that disabled people whose care is capped don't have to go to nursing homes. They can make up the difference by "paying for a few hours of care themselves," or by "encouraging neighbors, friends, or volunteers to assist in care."

But in Terri Desjardin's case, because of her parents' age and declining health, going to a nursing home seems like a real possibility. This scares the Desjardins.

"She has started going to school several nights a week, and doing well, and she really fears that's going to come to an end," says Martha. "It just seems cruel. It would be such a loss for her. And it's not just us. It's a whole lot of people. I realize that there's not enough money to go around. But there's an awful lot of young people who are going to be hurt by it. A lot of them are like Terri. They're just getting started, going back to school. They're in their own apartments and now they have to give that up."

The Inside of a Nursing Home

Maureen Griffin takes me on a tour of City View. "Just walking through, you can see how a young person might not want to live here," she says.

Residents sleep two to a room, in hospital beds with a curtain between them. The rooms are sunny but institutional, with gray tile floors and an antiseptic smell. A brightly colored calendar in the hall lists the day's activities: bingo, coffee hour, and Lawrence Welk.

City View's residents are quite elderly. Eight of them are sitting around the lounge area in wheelchairs, staring off in different directions. A soap opera is on the TV at the front of the room, but no one seems to be watching. Several women perk up when Griffin walks by, and she chats with them about getting their hair done, and about their health problems. Today is "hug day," Griffin explains. One resident hugs me and has me write my name on the heart-shaped card where she's collecting the signatures of her hug buddies.

"Some of these institutions don't look that bad. But keep in mind what it's like if you're twenty-two or twenty-five years old, and you're thinking about spending the rest of your life there," Bob Deist, the director of personal-care services at Access to Independence, says about nursing homes.

Even in City View's "Altercare" wing, where residents have private rooms and the atmosphere—a converted farm house—is more homey, it's extremely quiet. It's hard to imagine having friends over, hanging out, turning up the radio.

"We had a guy in here once who liked listening to loud music. He came in wearing a rock T-shirt," Griffin says, smiling. "He said he didn't like the aged population, even though he was sixty-nine years old himself." Ultimately, he went to a veterans' home, she says, where he apparently fit in better.

> *"[Nursing homes are] not geared toward helping people lead active lives outside the institution."*

According to a letter sent to home-care providers by the Department of Health and Social Services, the "small percentage of people having to enter nursing homes" because of the state's home-care cap, will be "free to leave the nursing home for work, education, and social events."

But disabled people and their advocates are extremely skeptical. Many have heard horror stories about nursing homes.

"Some people are terrified because they've been in nursing homes and they have not done well," says Froemming. "They've had recurrent respiratory infections, bedsores, or they've been left without bathing for a week."

Even a relatively pleasant place like City View, with a friendly, empathetic staff, is not geared toward helping people lead active lives outside the institution. "We've never had someone here who's going to school and working," says Griffin. "I wouldn't say it's impossible. But the leeway and flexibility they're used to having wouldn't be there."

Freedom vs. Costs

The price of freedom for some people with disabilities is just too high, the state legislature has decided. It's time to set priorities.

According to Angela Dombrowicki, chief of the policy section of the Bureau of Health Care Financing, the cap on home care "puts some kind of rationality in the system and sets some limits. With home-care services, there really are no incentives to limit spending on care. This is a first step toward a more managed system."

Medicaid rolls are indeed expanding at record rates. Between 1996 and 2001, Medicaid enrollment across the nation is expected to rise by 21 percent. Legislators are proposing caps, managed care, and other efforts to deal with the growing expense. Meanwhile, record numbers of people are still uninsured. There's no question that there's a health-care crisis.

"We need to get health costs under control, and we need to look at quality," says Edith Rasell, an economist at the Economic Policy Institute in Washington, D.C. "But you're not going to fix the problems with the health-care system by attacking Medicare and Medicaid. We need a comprehensive health-care solution, and nobody is even talking about that."

In the end, Wisconsin isn't going to save very much money with the home-care cap. For each of the next two fiscal years, the Bureau of Health Care Financing projects it will save $5,686,500 out of a total annual Medicaid budget of $2.4 billion, or about 0.2 percent—not much, considering the agony of the people affected.

Still, there is the question of priorities. Although up to now Medicaid has been "an open-ended entitlement" by the state's definition, there is not enough home care to go around. Because of a shortage of personal-care workers, the Medicaid personal-care program can't serve everyone who wants help. Medicaid also doesn't cover services like laundry and grocery shopping that the elderly and disabled need in order to live in the community. So, in 1982, the state created the Community Options Program for people at risk of going into nursing homes. Community Options pays for some things that Medical Assistance doesn't cover. But, unlike Medicaid, it is not an entitlement program. It only serves a fraction of the people who apply. According to the state, capping care for the most expensive clients will free up slots for people with less expensive needs.

> *"You're not going to fix the problems with the health-care system by attacking Medicare and Medicaid."*

In 1994 there were more than 1,100 people on the waiting list for Community Options just in Dane County. The elderly and the disabled are often pitted against each other, competing for slots. The Department of Health and Social Services estimates that, statewide, between 300 and 500 people on the waiting list can be served once Community Options stops serving people who exceed the cap.

But the program's administrators, who are still dealing with an inadequate pool of funds, are not thrilled about the trade-off. "It's a major change in state policy," says Francis Genter, who runs the Community Options Program in Dane County. "In the past, the *average* cost of the program had to be lower than the average cost of institutional care. But certain individuals could have more expensive care. Now, certain people with really high needs will never be eligible again."

Disabled people and their advocates have complained that it is unjust to single out people whose home care is expensive.

"It's not fair," says Verridan. "It's cheaper to be out in the community, when you add all the 'high-cost people' and 'low-cost people' together." But the state is comparing high-cost care in the community to average-cost nursing-home care.

"The only thing not capped is nursing homes," says Bob Deist. "That's the institutional bias."

Over the long haul, institutional care is also very expensive. Because of this, some people don't believe the state will save money with the cap. "I'm not sure it is a savings at all," says state representative Doris Hanson, who has helped introduce a bill to repeal the cap. "The Community Options Program has been very successful in terms of keeping people in their homes and saving money."

Making Do with Less

In the near-term, however, setting caps may work as a cost-cutting measure, if only because disabled people are determined to stay out of nursing homes, whatever the personal cost.

"People are so averse to the idea of going to nursing homes, they are accepting the cutbacks in care and patching things together with friends and volunteers and family members," says the Coalition for Advocacy's Froemming. "It's not clear how long that can hold up."

"I have some constituents who are making do with less," says Representative Hanson. "They're trying to go without some important health care to stay in the community, and that's a real concern."

What worries Francis Genter is that, as the state sets priorities for health care, giving people the most independent and rewarding life possible is no longer the primary concern. Since the creation of the Community Options Program in 1982, when it was hailed as a way of cutting costs *and* helping people lead independent lives, the state has done an ideological 180. Now the legislature seems intent on pushing people toward institutions.

"Cost is out front. Quality of life for citizens takes a back seat," says Genter. "It's a major value judgment to require people to move to institutional settings because their costs are high. I know how much people want to live in the place of their choice. These institutions are a long way from home."

Institutions Are Sometimes Necessary

by Voice of the Retarded

About the author: *Voice of the Retarded is an advocacy organization for persons with mental retardation and their relatives.*

A March 11, 1996, article in the *Washington Post* ("Move to Close Virginia Institutions for the Retarded Concerns Some Parents," Eric Lipton) posed this question: Do the remaining institutions have any role in society?

Voice of the Retarded (VOR) strongly opposes total deinstitutionalization, and therefore, answers the above question in the affirmative: Institutions for the mentally retarded are serving a critical role in the care of some mentally retarded individuals.

The Danger of Deinstitutionalizing

The national effort to deinstitutionalize and to create a single option of care (the community) for all individuals is threatening our most severely mentally disabled citizens. In addition to their severe mental limitations, many are also medically fragile. They require the type of care that can most effectively be provided in the stability of public and private developmental centers, which offer centralized medical, dental, rehabilitative and recreational care. The current system of care that has been established in community residential settings is not usually equipped to meet their complex needs. Until such a system is in place, advocates for deinstitutionalization are acting prematurely and are endangering the lives of these fragile human beings.

Two studies out of the University of California-Riverside emphasize the danger of closing all institutions. In one, Dr. David Strauss concludes that *retarded children were 25 percent more likely to die in their own homes or group homes* than they were in institutions. The other study reveals that *risk-adjusted mortality rates were 72 percent higher in the community* than in *institutions* for adults with developmental disabilities over the age of 40. These statistics are alarming, but not surprising. Again, most community residential settings do not offer a centralized

From Voice of the Retarded, "Statement on Deinstitutionalization," 1996. Reprinted with permission.

system of necessary medical care. Instead, many community residential settings are staffed with underpaid, inexperienced employees not trained to handle the complex medical and care needs of the clients being transferred from institutional settings. These conditions lead to high employee turn-over which precludes stability and continuity for those whose well-being often depends on care by persons intimately familiar with their particular needs.

Given these findings, why then is deinstitutionalization being pursued by other national organizations purporting to advocate on behalf of persons with mental retardation? Profit seems to be a motivating factor. Institutions are targeted as being an expensive option of care, and allegations are made that the same level of care can be provided for less in the community. Again, facts illustrate otherwise. A 1994 New Jersey study concluded that "the closing of developmental centers and private institutions would bring little savings and even added costs if specialized group home and day training services are the community options of choice." In another study in 1995, Dr. Peter Dobkin Hall revealed the fraudulent nature of the group home industry and community-based services in Connecticut. Finally, a 1993 U.S. House of Representatives Subcommittee report by former Representative Ron Wyden revealed "A disturbing pattern of abuse, neglect and fiscal mismanagement" in community living arrangements for mentally retarded persons. Statistics and studies aside, it simply makes common sense that the level of required medical care provided in one place would cost less than that same level of care provided in many different places scattered throughout a city—*and that level of care must not be compromised.*

> *"The national effort to deinstitutionalize . . . is threatening our most severely mentally disabled citizens."*

Many Needs, Many Options

The debate surrounding deinstitutionalization takes on many forms. Phrases such as "dignity of risk," "full inclusion" and "mainstreaming" are heard. As stated above, for many of the national organizations pushing for deinstitutionalization, the bottom line is profit. For others, including members of the general public, deinstitutionalization is embraced due to the large amounts of incomplete and inaccurate information being disseminated by some of those who stand to profit. Why else would proponents for deinstitutionalization be pushing for a single option of care for a population made up of individuals with so many different needs? Why else would proponents for deinstitutionalization work so hard to eliminate services when thousands of individuals with mental retardation remain unserved on waiting lists in every state?

Total deinstitutionalization is no more sound than total institutionalization. Persons with mental retardation have distinct needs and we must not deny them their right to be individuals. This right includes choice and access to proper supports.

One size does not fit all.

Cash Grants for Disabled Children Are Essential

by Mary Somoza

About the author: *Mary Somoza is a member of the New York State Advisory Council of the Office of Mental Retardation and Developmental Disabilities.*

One of the best-kept secrets of the welfare reform legislation [The Personal Responsibility Act of 1995] passed by the House of Representatives in March 1995 and passed in May 1995 by the Senate Finance Committee is the virtual decimation of the Supplemental Security Income program for children with severe disabilities. [The Personal Responsibility Act (HR 4) was vetoed by President Bill Clinton on January 9, 1996.]

This Federal program provides cash assistance of up to $458 a month to 900,000 low-income families to cover some of the costs of raising their children at home rather than in foster care, group homes or institutions. If the legislation goes through, 225,000 children—18,000 in New York State—would lose their benefits within six months.

Essential Aid for Families

This program has kept my family together. In 1983, my twin daughters, Alba and Anastasia, were born prematurely and diagnosed with cerebral palsy. Both needed around-the-clock care. My husband is a self-employed photographer, and we did not have medical insurance when they arrived. In less than a year, we were bankrupted by the girls' enormous medical bills. Our family then became eligible for the Supplemental Security Income program because of the severity of the twins' condition.

In New York, like many states, the program enables children with severe disabilities to enroll in Medicaid. And the cash assistance, though relatively small, was also crucial. Because the twins both have severe quadriplegia and use heavy custom-designed wheelchairs, the many hospital appointments they required meant large outlays of cash for transportation.

Unlike most families who can rely on public transportation, it is virtually impossible to travel anywhere lugging two wheelchairs weighing about 160 pounds each. But with assistance from the program, eventually we were able to pay for our own van, and could afford insurance coverage, maintenance and parking. The van allows my children to get to all of their medical appointments, play at friends' houses and participate in after-school events just like other children.

We also needed cash assistance since we can't have a teen-ager or a regular babysitter look after our children but must pay a person trained in working with children with severe disabilities. And the twins' custom wheelchair equipment, braces and feeding tubes are a big expense.

Contrary to popular belief, not everything is covered by Medicaid. In any case, the needs of growing children are immediate and can't always wait for the lengthy approval process Medicaid requires.

The Myth of Widespread Abuse

Some reports have led members of Congress to believe that widespread abuse of the Supplemental Security Income program is common—that families coach children to "act crazy" in order to appear eligible for disability benefits. But when investigated by three separate agencies—the Social Security Administration, the General Accounting Office and the Department of Health and Human Services—in 1995 these charges were found to be completely unsubstantiated.

Nevertheless, zealous budget-cutters led Congress to believe that access to the program was easy. In fact, the opposite is true. Our family

> *"In less than a year, we were bankrupted by the girls' enormous medical bills."*

endured exhaustive interviews, medical tests and intrusive scrutiny of our financial records when we applied for the Supplemental Security Income program in 1984. Never before had we received any Government aid, and many times my husband and I almost gave up because the process was so difficult. But the thought that our children might be institutionalized gave us the strength to continue. After four months of intense investigation, we were approved.

I used to feel that my case was particularly compelling because I had twins with such severe disabilities. Over the years, however, I have met many parents whose children look "normal" to others yet suffer from serious mental disabilities.

Such parents are under constant stress, often facing day and night supervision of their children. While their children's problems are completely different than my children's, they experience many of the difficulties I do, and sometimes more. Yet these families face elimination from the program. . . .

Too High a Price

Despite the physical, emotional and financial demands placed on my husband and me, our twins are an integral part of our family. We love them and do not want to be separated from them.

But if the support that families like mine now receive from the Supplemental Security Income program is taken away, many of us will be unable to raise our children and will have to put them in institutions. This would cost taxpayers more money, and I can't imagine what it would do to the families. It is a price no one should ever have to pay.

Cash Grants for Disabled Children Have Been Abused

by LynNell Hancock

About the author: *LynNell Hancock is a general editor at* Newsweek.

It's a federal program crafted with the most generous of intentions: to help severely disabled children living in poverty. Supplemental Security Income (SSI) money could pay for day care, extra utility bills, wheelchairs. For nearly 20 years, however, only the most extreme cases received the aid, which averaged about $400 a month. Then, in 1990, the U.S. Supreme Court decided that too many kids who needed help were being left out of the money. Since then, thousands of kids who needed federal help got it. But even this act of civic decency did not remain uncorrupted. An army of parents has marched on schools across the land demanding that their children be tagged disabled so they can reap the financial rewards of a monthly check. This remarkable mixture of public generosity and private greed has led to demands that the program undergo radical reforms again. The question now is whether children in need will suffer for the sins of other fathers.

Scam Stories and "Crazy Checks"

The scam stories are legion. A 16-year-old Milwaukee girl, once a good student, begins to act up, get poor grades and arrive at class with wads of gum stuck in her hair. She is finally labeled learning-impaired. Her low-income family starts receiving federal disability checks. Only, her parents use the money to pay for a van, a stereo and a Florida vacation. In a nearby suburb, two children with minor speech and attention disorders receive cash every month but still come to school with eyeglasses so scratched they can't see. Other parents refuse to administer Ritalin medication to their hyperactive offspring, for fear the monthly subsidies would cease if the kids get well. And in Beloit, Wis., a school psychologist says a mother of five is coaching all her children to "act crazy" in order to qualify for aid. When a teacher asks the woman's 9-year-old son why he is so relentlessly disruptive, he replies, "If I get better, my mother will beat me, because we need the crazy money."

This sad scramble for "crazy checks," as they're known on the street, has triggered media and government investigations. Lawmakers point with concern to the rising number of children receiving the checks—up from 296,000 to 800,000 in four years. Spending, in turn, rose from $1.2 billion to $4.5 billion. But a closer look at the numbers and cases shows that the cheating, while odious, may not be widespread. A recent inspector general's report from the Department of Health and Human Services indicates only 1 percent of the flimflam artists actually succeeded in using their kids to jack up their bank accounts. Most of the worst-case abuse stories never make it past the application stage. At least 750,000 requests for SSI for children who cannot function in "an age-appropriate manner," as the regulations say, were rejected between 1992 and 1994.

> *"Parents [are] demanding that their children be tagged disabled so they can reap the financial rewards of a monthly check."*

Parents' Reactions

The long odds have not kept parents from trying to bully their way into the federal candy store. One Chicago mother keeps her healthy child home from school, claiming he is on medication, in order to bolster her case for SSI. "She is determined to make her child an invalid," says Pat Tamburrino, assistant principal at the Funston school. Another mother in the same school on the city's northwest side tried three times to prove her seventh-grade daughter, a star cheerleader, was disabled by asthma. Once, she removed her from the cheerleading squad. Next, she provided a doctor's note saying the asthma was so bad her daughter couldn't tie her shoes. "What I'm seeing here is an abuse of the system," says Tamburrino. "The word has spread."

For those parents who really do have kids with serious problems, the checks can mean the difference between keeping children at home and farming them out to institutions. "Because it's a cash grant, the family can meet the needs of these children as they exist," says Jonathan M. Stein, general counsel at Philadelphia's Community Legal Services, Inc., who argued the Supreme Court case that redefined the law. One family may need to build a ramp, while another needs a toilet. A North Carolina mother used her SSI checks to install indoor plumbing after years of carrying her paralyzed child to the outhouse. Conni and Lynn Guyer of Dayton, Ohio, paid for private school for their 13-year-old son, Nathan, who suffers from afflictions that include a severe attention-deficit hyperactivity disorder. His special-education teachers had given up on his ever learning to read, says Conni. He was depressed and "virtually suicidal." The SSI money pays for a special school for the learning-disabled, where Nathan is finally thriving. "It's turned his life around," says his mother. "I have a different child."

Mending the Loopholes

Still, critics charge that children with learning problems are already entitled to expensive special-education services in public school that include speech therapy in mild cases, on-site nurses in the more severe. Medicaid provides for other medical needs. Children with behavior problems, the new category on SSI's rolls, have quadrupled in four years. "This has the potential to become a big sucking black hole," says Cynthea Rollo, a school psychologist in the Milwaukee suburb of Waukesha. "If taxpayers were aware of some of these cases, there would be an uprising." But it is no mystery why the number of applications rose so dramatically. The court ordered the Social Security Administration to advertise the new eligibility regulations and pay retroactive lump sums. Large cities are actively urging people to switch from Aid to Families with Dependent Children to SSI because it saves local dollars. AFDC is funded partly by local money. SSI is strictly federal. New York City, for example, saved $1.4 million in two years from its AFDC welfare rolls.

Not even its staunchest defenders believe the system isn't riddled with holes. Rep. Gerald Kleczka of Milwaukee is at the forefront of SSI reform. He plans to introduce a bill that could curtail the wide array of children with behavioral problems now receiving money. "I'd say close to 50 percent could be saved if we tighten the criteria," says Kleczka, who helped win the battle to put a three-year cap on the amount of time alcohol- and drug-addicted adults can receive SSI. The liberal Democrat is looking into improving monitoring and replacing cash with vouchers, to ensure that the money is spent on the child's condition. Social Security Administration Commissioner Shirley Chater says she welcomes reform. "If a child is labeled disabled at the age of 9, it can be a self-fulfilling prophecy," she says. "I would like to see incentives for children to pursue a high quality of life."

> *"If I get better, my mother will beat me, because we need the crazy money."*

Chapter 3

Should Disabled Children Be Mainstreamed?

Mainstreaming: An Overview

by Susan Chira

About the author: *Susan Chira is a reporter for the* New York Times.

Merari Vazquez's fellow second and third graders are learning about perimeters. Measuring is hard for Merari, who is mentally retarded and does not speak. But she is part of the group, and her classmates need to find a way she can work with them. They coax her to lie down on a big pad, using her to do their measuring.

A Controversial Experiment

Merari is part of a bold but hotly debated educational experiment: teaching even severely handicapped children in regular public school classrooms instead of separate ones. The idea goes far beyond "mainstreaming," which usually involves milder disabilities; at schools like Merari's, no heads turn at children using wheelchairs, feeding tubes or oxygen tanks.

Schools like those in Johnson City, in south-central New York, are rare; no one keeps a nationwide count. But experts say their number is growing. And as it grows, the movement toward "inclusion" is dividing advocates for disabled children. Some hail it as an ethical and educational breakthrough; others believe children's individual needs are being sacrificed in a crusade.

At schools in places like Johnson City and Redmond, Wash.—which pay for extra aides, special education teachers to modify lessons and teacher training—children with disabilities from autism to Down's syndrome are flourishing socially and educationally. Their classmates, too, learn empathy and tolerance for those who are different. Moreover, because many schools use the money they would have spent on special education classes to pay for the extra help the disabled students need in regular schools, inclusion does not have to cost more.

But some studies show that in schools that offer inclusion programs with little extra help to these students, children are failing. Some children, particularly those with emotional problems, put terrible strains on regular classrooms; others may need the smaller, quieter and more individual settings of special education. And inclusion seems to be a daunting task in inner cities, where many teachers face overcrowded classrooms already full of troubled children.

"I'm very pro-inclusion on a philosophical basis, but it isn't working well," said James Ysseldyke, a professor at the University of Minnesota who worked to introduce inclusion in schools in Minneapolis as part of a four-year Federally financed project. "It's being used with every good intention to do some terrible things to kids."

Making Inclusion Work

Johnson City is a small, largely blue-collar suburb of Binghamton with 3,000 children enrolled in its four schools. The school district has been innovative for 20 years, recognized by the Education Department as a national model, both for its students' consistently high test scores and its creative teaching methods. Since 1986, Johnson City has moved all but 14 of its nearly 200 special education students to regular classrooms; as many as 10 percent of the students in any given class may be disabled in some way.

Though no one knows exactly how many schools like Johnson City's there are now nationwide, partly because there are so many forms of inclusion, they are clearly reaching thousands of children. In the 1989–90 school year, the last year for which figures were available, 6 percent of children with multiple disabilities and 6.7 percent of mentally retarded children, for example, were in regular classrooms, according to the Education Department.

But statistics can be misleading, particularly because states or schools with very low percentages of children in special education do not say whether disabled students receive extra services in regular classrooms.

In New York City, where 15,000 students with severe disabilities are taught in separate schools, 30 are being placed in regular kindergarten and first-grade classrooms in six schools as part of an experimental program.

> *"Some hail [inclusion] as an ethical and educational breakthrough; others believe children's individual needs are being sacrificed."*

Johnson City schools are full of sights that in other schools would be extraordinary. Some of the desks have charts with letters and numbers, for children who cannot speak and need to point to communicate.

A classmate casually tucks C.J. Shearn's books in the back of his wheelchair as C.J. rolls himself to his next sixth-grade class, pausing as other students slap him five. When Bobby Westcott needs to stop playing to breathe with his oxygen tank, his kindergarten classmates matter-of-factly take a break, too.

At the Emily Dickinson School in Redmond, an affluent suburb of Seattle, Andy Heilman, 12, plans to share a bunk at summer camp with Cameron

Archibald, who cannot read or write, must be fed through a tube and suffers from seizures. The other day, when Cameron was upset at having to leave class to return a book to the library, Andy took his arm. "I'll be here when you get back, okay, Cam?" Andy said.

Such comfort and friendliness do not come automatically. Students in Redmond were given training in sensitivity before the special-education students entered their classrooms.

Lori Sinicki, a special education teacher who teaches in inclusive classrooms at Johnson City Senior High School, says it is attitudes like these that set Johnson City apart. "We're demystifying disabilities," she said. "But we don't just say we're putting kids in the classroom for socialization. There has to be learning going on."

Indeed, a study of the district by Christine Salisbury, then a professor at the State University of New York at Binghamton, found that test scores of both disabled and regular students continued to rise over a three-year period after they were put in the same classes. She has not measured beyond that period.

To make sure all children learn, Mrs. Sinicki and other special education teachers work closely with regular teachers. Disabled children are placed with others their own age. The teachers change teaching materials, making tapes of books for children who have trouble reading or adding maps and charts for children who need a visual presentation of information. They alter tests, making some multiple choice so that children who cannot write can point to the right answers. Teachers set different goals for different students; some might get top grades if they learn part of the material.

> *"In the 1989–90 school year, . . . 6 percent of children with multiple disabilities and 6.7 percent of mentally retarded children . . . were in regular classrooms."*

Parents say they are delighted. Pat Poliziano's son Andrew, who has multiple handicaps, spoke his first words and made friends in his first-grade class at Lincoln Elementary School in Johnson City. "He progresses better when he has an example," she said. "When we were kids, they trotted kids like him into a special bus and they were never put on view."

The Perils of Mainstreaming

But a large chorus of skeptics say that the successes in Johnson City and Redmond are the shining exceptions to a dismal rule. These are small, relatively homogeneous and innovative districts. But in most schools, they say, inclusion in practice means depositing children in regular classrooms without extra help for them or specially trained teachers.

"Take the teacher where 20 percent of her kids speak Spanish, 10 percent Hmong; she's got 37 kids in her classroom now. Talk to her about including a kid who needs an aide, and she'll look at you crosswise," said Dr. Mary Wagner, director of the National Longitudinal Transition Study of Special Education Students, the largest such study of students' academic results.

Her study of high schools found that while disabled students in regular classrooms made more friends and fitted better into groups, the longer they spent in regular classrooms, the more likely they were to fail and drop out. For example, 61 percent of students who had learning disabilities failed at least one class when placed in regular education, as against 14 percent who remained in special education classes.

> *"The debate over inclusion is consuming the politically active special education community."*

Dr. Wagner and many other advocates for disabled children worry that the inclusion movement will mean that these children will lose what is theirs by Federal law—the legal right to get special services and the extra money needed to pay for them. With schools under financial pressure, these advocates worry that districts will abolish special education as an economizing device and fail to put the money into support services.

The 1975 law establishing handicapped children's rights to special services called for placing such children in regular classrooms whenever possible, but including a "continuum of services," or a range of programs, including separate schools and separate small classes offering individual help. Several organizations for disabled children, including the nation's largest, the Council for Exceptional Children, say they support inclusion whenever sensible, but insist on keeping separate classes for those children who need them.

"Inclusion doesn't make sense for all kids," Professor Ysseldyke said.

Even in Johnson City, there are dissenters. Howard Rhodes, a special education counselor, says he believes in the ideal of inclusion but adds that some children do not benefit from it.

To do a better job, he said, the district should offer many more services, including full-time psychiatrists, family counseling and remedial classes.

Dr. Ed Martin, president of the National Center for Disability Services in Albertson, Long Island, and a chief architect of the 1975 law, says he has come to believe that separate schools for disabled children have the same legitimacy as historically black colleges.

Making School Hospitable

The debate over inclusion is consuming the politically active special education community, with true believers on each side. But for many parents, particularly those whose children did not thrive in special education, inclusion offers hope that schools can be changed so they are more hospitable places for their children.

Mary Roadcap, who works as an aide in Johnson City, has a disabled son who dropped out of school. "If my son had been at this place," she said, "he wouldn't have felt inferior." She spent her day helping Darran Caswell, a fourth grader who could not speak and has trouble walking. When children spoke to her, she gently told them that Darran could hear them. She coaxed Darran to participate in the measuring class, and praised him when he lay down on the pad by himself.

"Other school systems don't know what to do with a child who's a little different," she said. "If I can help one person here, it's enough, because nobody cared about my son."

Mainstreaming Can Be Effective

by Ray Van Dyke, Martha Ann Stallings, and Kenna Colley

About the authors: *Ray Van Dyke is the principal of Kipps Elementary School in Blacksburg, Virginia. Martha Ann Stallings is a fifth-grade teacher at Kipps. Kenna Colley is an inclusion specialist at Kipps.*

Inclusion is a philosophy that acknowledges the importance of the real world for students' learning. Every society has had to face the question of how to treat individuals who differ from the norm, and the vision of building strong communities based on peace, unity, and acceptance for all is an appealing one. We can begin to make this vision a reality in our public schools by accepting and valuing children with disabilities exactly as they are.

Children's Community

Schools are the communities to which children belong in their most formative years. Classrooms reflect real life with its challenges and distractions. Children with disabilities need to be immersed in this microcosm of the "real world," beginning in preschool and continuing throughout their educational careers. This is the "normal" world that they will be required to live and work in, so their education ought to take place in classrooms that reflect that world. To be truly prepared to take part in the real world as adults, children with disabilities need to be educated in language-rich classrooms and to interact daily with peers who are appropriate role models.

Full inclusion occurs when a child with a disability learns in a general education classroom alongside his or her agemates with all the necessary supports. These supports are provided through extensive teamwork and communication. Moreover, in providing these supports, schools must always consider the best interests of the student with disabilities, his or her peers, and all the members of the inclusion team, including the special educator, the general educator, parents, building administrators, therapists, and other support personnel.

Abridged from Ray Van Dyke, Martha Ann Stallings, and Kenna Colley, "How to Build an Inclusive School Community: A Success Story," *Phi Delta Kappan*, February 1995. Reprinted with permission.

Whatever else it may be, inclusion should *never* be seen as a money-saving option for a school or district. Under inclusion, no support services are taken away from students; indeed, even more support may be required to enable a student to function optimally in the general education classroom. In addition, all members of the inclusion team will need training, and that training should continue as long as the child with special needs is included in the general classroom. An individual child's educational program is developed and owned by all team members. There is not a single expert, but a team of experts who contribute interdependently to each child's program.

The Basis for Inclusion

We base our support for the philosophy of inclusion on three fundamental arguments. First, we believe that inclusion has a legal base. The great majority of court cases have not upheld the traditional practice of segregating students with special educational needs. Many cases are still pending, but it is unusual to pick up an education journal today without seeing some reference to inclusion and the legal mandates that support the practice. The bottom line of the argument for inclusion is that each child has a legal right to an equal opportunity to obtain an education in the "least restrictive environment" possible. For many advocates of inclusion, the fight for inclusion has become a civil rights issue in that segregated programs are seen to be inherently unequal and a violation of the rights of students with special educational needs.

A second argument for inclusion rests on the results of research on best practices. Research continues to show that students who are not pulled out do better than those who are segregated. Analyses of segregated special education programs indicate that they have simply not worked. Despite increases in spending and the growth of the special education bureaucracy, children in segregated special education programs have not shown the growth that was predicted. Indeed, in many locales students have been sorted and selected to the point that a classroom teacher rarely has an entire class together at any point during the day. Substitutes sometimes find that their greatest challenge is knowing which students are supposed to be where at which times. From simple observation we have found that students benefit from staying in one room for most of the day.

"Full inclusion occurs when a child with a disability learns in a general education classroom alongside his or her agemates."

Finally, but perhaps most important, a strong moral and ethical argument can be made for the "rightness" of inclusion: it is the best thing to do for the students. Segregating students throughout the day in any way is not good: it classifies, it creates bias, and it makes them different. Schools are a reflection of the communities they serve, and so all members of those communities should be a part of the schools. Students with special needs are a part of our communities, and, with the inclusion philosophy, we can make them more and more a part of our school communities. We need to learn from one another in our schools so that we can do the same in our communities. In the future, students majoring in education are likely to regard the practice of segregating students with special needs in much the same way as we look upon racial segregation before the 1960s. It will be seen as an embarrassing chapter of our education history.

The Role of the Special Education Teacher

When inclusion was first initiated in some school systems, the myth existed that special educators would no longer be needed since the children once taught in separate classrooms would be in general education classrooms. This is very far from the truth. Indeed, the role of the special educator is crucial.

The special educator can act as the case manager for his or her students, facilitating team meetings and planning sessions. He or she is responsible for determining the curricular adaptations that may need to be in place on a daily or weekly basis and for facilitating the development by parents and team members of an individualized education program (IEP). In addition, the special educator documents the fulfillment of the IEP throughout the year and is usually the liaison with the therapists.

The special educator should also be involved in actively developing and participating in planning and support sessions involving the classmates of the child with a disability. These sessions are necessary to the success of the child who is included. Peers need

> *"Each child has a legal right to an equal opportunity to obtain an education in the 'least restrictive environment' possible."*

to understand the unique aspects of their classmate; to learn facts, not myths; to learn how to interact with their classmate; and to develop empathy and respect for that person. The job description could literally go on and on, but the most important role the special educator takes on is that of team player, especially in supporting the classroom teacher.

Inclusion does not mean that a child never receives separate instruction in skills or functional routines. However, if a child is to receive separate instruction, it should be a valuable experience that can only be done outside the classroom. For example, if a child needs intensive reading instruction in a small group or even one-to-one, this instruction should be built into his or her schedule at an appropriate time (e.g., during the language arts period). Such specialized instruction may be provided by a general educator, a special educator, or an instructional assistant. But all such instruction should be meaningful and necessary. Too often students are "pulled out" of their classrooms to learn skills that will not help them function better in any environment.

Some educators argue that students with significant physical disabilities or with intellectual disabilities cannot learn functional life skills in a general education environment. If a student needs to work on toileting skills, the type of classroom he or she is in makes no difference. Bathrooms can be found in the school building, and these skills can be worked on there at natural or scheduled times of the day. Similar advice ap-plies for mealtime skills, grooming skills, and many other skills that may be priority areas on some children's IEPs. Community living and voca-tional skills can also be a part of stu-dent's schedules, as long as they are skills that the parents and team mem-

> *"Students in an inclusive setting develop a new sense of understanding and respect for one another and for human differences."*

bers have identified as being necessary and relevant. Usually, for students in primary and elementary grades, the school building is their community, and trips off school grounds are not necessary.

We have also had the opportunity to work with included children who face behavioral challenges. This is the most controversial and unsettling aspect of inclusion. No matter what environment a child is in, behavioral challenges are constant and time-consuming. This is nothing new to public schools or to spe-cial educators. The fact is, if you put a group of children together who demon-strate challenging behaviors, those behaviors will tend to increase and become more intense through imitation and an effort to attract more attention.

If you wait for a child to be "ready" to move into an inclusive setting by expect-ing his or her behaviors to improve in a segregated environment, that day may never come. The "readiness theory" is a myth. Children with challenging behav-iors need positive role models, structure, and specific behavioral plans based on natural rewards and contingencies that are designed to replace negative behaviors with positive ones. This takes a great deal of teamwork, flexibility, and determi-nation on the part of all staff members. However, the rewards are worth the effort.

Peers are the most important part of planning for a student who exhibits chal-lenging behaviors. Peers need to understand why the behaviors are occurring and to brainstorm and plan for ways to help their classmate. This kind of involvement gives students the chance to learn to depend on one another. Children learn to work together, to plan, and to put their plans into action. Such skills are valuable throughout a lifetime and cannot be learned from any textbook.

The Role of the Classroom Teacher

To be successful in an inclusive setting, a general education teacher must be-lieve that students with disabilities can learn successfully and deserve the op-portunity to learn in age-appropriate classrooms. We continue to celebrate the abundant learning that takes place among classmates of all abilities in class-rooms throughout our school. We see students with disabilities learning along-side their nondisabled peers in an environment in which support is provided and a real feeling of community exists.

Students in an inclusive setting develop a new sense of understanding and respect for one another and for human differences. Classroom teachers who do not lower their expectations continue to be amazed at what students can achieve in a risk-free environment where differences are recognized and celebrated. Students feel very comfortable with the idea that everyone has something to offer. Members of the class get to know one another, talk about likes and dislikes, and start to realize that they are all equal members of the classroom community. In such a classroom, individual needs are met, from the needs of the student who has been identified as a gifted learner to those of the student who has an IEP that requires specific support and accommodations.

There are many components to such a community classroom, and, more important, we have found that strategies that are effective for inclusion tend to benefit all learners, regardless of their abilities or disabilities.

Effective discipline strategies must be in place, and part of any successful discipline strategy is the setting of realistic and positive goals for students. With realistic goals in place for individuals, appropriate classroom behaviors thrive. When students recognize the appropriateness of their own behaviors, they become more trustworthy and confident.

Cooperative learning is a noncompetitive teaching strategy that works well in an inclusive classroom. Through the activities of cooperative learning groups, each student can play an equal part in classroom activity. The roles of group members need to be defined clearly, and all members of the group must participate, allowing each student to make a contribution to the learning process.

> *"Strategies that are effective for inclusion tend to benefit all learners."*

Thus the roles of individual group members are clearly important, and each student can feel valued—even as a student develops needed interpersonal skills.

Therefore, from the first day of school the classroom teacher must take ownership of included students with special needs. These students are no longer thought of as the special education teacher's students who have been placed in a general education classroom for a short period. The classroom teacher should become very involved with the process of developing the IEP and with making sure that the necessary supports and services are provided to the included student. The students feel a real sense of belonging in such an environment. . . .

Different Abilities, Same Goals

A very important part of allowing each student to participate actively at his or her own level and to meet individualized goals is an overlapping curriculum. Offering different materials on the same topic but at different reading levels has proved to be very successful. The same curriculum goals are expected of all students, but differences are taken into account.

Parent involvement has proved vital in inclusive classrooms. Most often, if parents are informed of what is taking place in the classroom, they will be supportive. Parents can be invited to volunteer in the classroom, both to assist the teacher and to witness firsthand how he or she goes about meeting the individual needs of the students. When the classroom community is extended to include parents, greater involvement will lead to greater success.

Involving students as peer helpers for students with disabilities is a very effective strategy. Teachers will need to model strategies for students and allow students to be involved in problem-solving sessions. Peer assistance and support can help nondisabled students build and maintain relationships with their disabled peers. Classrooms in which diversity is valued can enrich the learning of all students involved.

> *"Involving students as peer helpers for students with disabilities is a very effective strategy."*

In a successful inclusive classroom, the general educator, the special educator, and any instructional assistants must collaborate to meet the needs of all students. For successful collaboration to take place, the following assets are key.

• *Communication.* Teachers who collaborate must be honest and open about concerns and feelings.

• *Flexibility.* Teachers in inclusive classrooms must be willing to "roll with the punches," to compromise, and to do things differently if necessary.

• *Shared ownership.* The student with an IEP is part of the general class and thus "belongs to" the general education teacher. The special education teacher plays a variety of roles that support the student and the classroom teacher.

• *Recognition of differing needs.* All students can successfully meet the same curriculum goals with adaptation and support appropriate to their individual needs.

• *Need-based instruction.* Collaborators must be willing to plan activities that ensure success and not be overly concerned with time lines.

• *Willingness to be a team player.* The team must be willing to plan and work together on all issues, especially student behavior.

• *Dependability.* Each team member must be prepared for his or her part of all planning and lesson responsibilities.

• *Cooperative grading.* The special education teacher and the general education teacher should evaluate students' progress together. Each must be responsible for his or her own part of the total evaluation.

• *IEP responsibility.* Both teachers must collaborate in writing the IEP, and they must be equal partners in carrying it out, though the special education teacher usually monitors progress.

• *Sense of humor.* Laugh a lot! Teachers must support each other with smiles, send notes of encouragement, and, most of all, share successes.

The Cost of Inclusion

Inclusion is *not* a program that a school system should consider as a way to save money. To do it right will cost more money. However, the payoffs for all students are likely to be worth the extra cost.

We have found that, in most cases, students with special needs who are included are achieving at far higher levels than they did in segregated classrooms. We have also found them blossoming socially, and many have developed real friendships with children in their neighborhoods. In addition, all students have benefited from having such extra supports as curricular adaptations, study aids, and more individualized assistance. All students are learning that everyone brings strengths and needs to every situation. They are learning about conflict resolution and the importance of being responsible.

Things that were stumbling blocks at first have become benefits. For example, greater collaboration among teachers and other staff members has allowed them to share skills and resources and has led to the improvement of all instruction. We no longer have regular education supplies and special education supplies. We simply have educational supplies, and money has been reallocated to reflect that. Moreover, we no longer have the need for a large fleet of special education buses to bus students out of their home attendance areas for a particular special education class.

Our school system did not increase funding during two years of inclusion; we operated on a frozen budget. Though costs have now increased as more schools in our division have begun to adopt inclusion, our per-pupil expenditures for students with special needs are still less than those of most neighboring school systems, especially those that bus students to other schools and those that pay tuition for students with special needs to attend schools in other districts.

We also found ways to reallocate resources, despite the fact that Virginia allocates special education funds categorically and not according to inclusion models. We have found that, through writing waivers, we can place teachers in cross-categorical positions so that they may consult from school to school on student needs. A cost comparison of self-contained versus inclusive programs in our system showed that, with the latter, money could be saved on classroom equipment, transportation, instructional materials, and mobile classrooms.

With the passage of the Americans with Disabilities Act and the continuing success stories emerging from inclusion programs around the country, we believe that our schools reflect a society that is ready to embrace *all* children, regardless of abilities or disabilities, so that they can be educated together and learn to value one another as unique individuals. Those schools that continue to struggle to keep students with disabilities out of general education classrooms should seriously consider investing their time, effort, and money instead in the creation of environments that welcome all students.

Mainstreaming Benefits All Students

by Diane Haas

About the author: *Diane Haas is an elementary school teacher in Champaign County, Ohio.*

A new phase of special education reform known as full inclusion began in the 1980s. Full inclusion is a term used to describe the placement of children with disabilities in a regular education classroom with children who do not have disabilities.

Special Education vs. Full Inclusion

The Education of the Handicapped Act enacted in 1975 (since renamed The Individuals with Disabilities Education Act) mandates that handicapped children, including children in public or private institutions, be educated with non-handicapped children. Handicapped children should be removed from the regular education classroom only when the nature and severity of the handicap is such that education cannot be achieved satisfactorily.

However, since the 1970s, children with disabilities have been removed from the regular classroom to a separate self-contained special education classroom for part of a school day. This approach was commonly referred to as the pull-out program.

Advocates of full inclusion argue that the practice of segregating children with disabilities from children without disabilities fails to serve the individualized needs of each student with disabilities. Such removal has resulted in a fragmented approach to special education. If the goal of special education is to help children with disabilities so that they can function in everyday society, these children must not be totally segregated from peers without disabilities. Direct observations of the behavior of students with disabilities in the regular class have suggested that their behavior resembles that of students without disabilities.

Diane Haas, "Inclusion Is Happening in the Classroom," *Children Today*, vol. 22, no. 3, 1993. Courtesy of the Administration for Children and Families, U.S. Dept. of Health and Human Services.

Teachers' and peers' perception of the academic ability and behavior of the student with disabilities has a great deal to do with that child's social acceptance. The appropriate place to develop social and communication skills is in regular education classes and activities in a normal school setting. Segregation promotes dependence and isolation and limits opportunities for students to learn skills that enhance independent living and social participation. When children with disabilities are isolated from regular students, it sends the message that they are different and cannot function in everyday society.

The Message of Inclusion

Inclusion really means less exclusion. Inclusion can be described as a belief that values each person as an important, accepted member of the school and/or community. The message of inclusion is that "I will meet you on your terms where you are." The concept of full inclusion is and always has been reflected in the federal and state requirement for serving students with disabilities in the least restrictive environment. Special education was never meant to be defined as a place, but rather was intended to be a specifically designed instruction provided at no cost to the parent.

In order for full inclusion to work, additional support in the form of human and/or fiscal resources must accompany the child with disabilities who is integrated into the regular education program. Inclusion means bringing the special education teacher as a resource and teammate into the regular class to help not only the child with disabilities but to help the rest of the children as well. While co-teaching, the special education teacher and the regular teacher plan lessons and deliver instruction together, and share the responsibility for assessing students' mastery. This results in an environment that is diverse and rich. One teacher might teach a large group while the other teacher circulates around the room, paying particular attention to the needs of students with disabilities.

The teachers might teach a subject together or divide the class in half, each teaching the same information to a smaller group. The special edu-

"Children with disabilities can teach children without disabilities valuable lessons."

cator can bring his or her resources and knowledge to a more natural setting, the regular classroom, where effective learning and behavior are supposed to occur. Through team teaching, students with disabilities avoid the stigma associated with daily journeys in and out of the classroom. In addition, the special education teacher is involved in the regular daily instruction. Students can benefit from having two teachers in the classroom who can provide extra help and more options for learning.

Schools that include all children in their regular classrooms have incorporated teachers, parents and administrators into teams. Parents are encouraged to meet with professionals on a regular basis, share responsibility, and develop meaningful relationships. Through a multidisciplinary approach, teachers, parents, administrators and related service providers recognize the complexity of the task at hand and organize personnel and resources in a manner that allows for success. Teaming provides a support network and a powerful problem-solving tool.

Valuable Lessons

How does the presence of students with special needs affect other students in the classroom? I believe that children with disabilities can teach children without disabilities valuable lessons. Some examples could be patience, the importance of trying hard to do your best, and the development of an understanding for children who learn differently. A healthy child may see that a child with disabilities can excel in certain areas. The extraordinary technological advances in devices to assist students with disabilities have vastly improved their ability to communicate and interact with and manipulate their environment. Segregated schools generally offer few, if any, opportunities for children with disabilities to interact with peers without disabilities, and thus these children are deprived of valuable learning and socialization experiences. Full inclusion can show children and adults the value of accepting people as they are and can demonstrate that children with disabilities are important individuals who can contribute to society.

Special Education Programs Have Failed

by Joseph P. Shapiro, Penny Loeb, and David Bowermaster

About the authors: *Joseph P. Shapiro is a senior editor, Penny Loeb is an associate editor, and David Bowermaster is a reporter/researcher for* U.S. News & World Report.

Billy Hawkins speaks softly as he tells his students of the promise of special education. "Every child," he says, "can learn." Billy Hawkins should know. For the first 15 years of his life, he was labeled by his teachers as "educable mentally retarded." That meant "special education"—and a stigma that too often in America was a passport to failure.

Things changed for Hawkins one crisp fall night in 1970. A backup quarterback, Hawkins came in off the bench and rallied his team from far behind. In the stands, the principal watched the high school sophomore in amazement. The "retarded kid" could play. He ran complicated plays; he clearly had a gift for the game. Soon after, the principal had Hawkins enrolled in regular classes, his teachers instructed to give him extra help. Today, Billy Hawkins is 39. He holds a Ph.D. and is the associate dean of the school of education at Michigan's Ferris State University.

The Exception to the Rule

It is an inspiring story, but in the world of special education, it is the exception, not the rule. Just a few years after Billy Hawkins moved out of a special classroom to rejoin the rest of his schoolmates, Congress passed a law requiring public schools to educate all children with disabilities. In the years since, the good intentions have yielded decidedly mixed results. While millions of American children have received educations as a result of the Individuals with Disabilities Education Act (IDEA), the school system created by the law hurts many of the very children it is intended to help even as it costs taxpayers billions.

A five-month examination of the nation's special education system by *U.S. News* has documented a network of programs that regularly use subjective testing criteria, that rely on funding formulas and identification procedures that funnel ever greater numbers of children into special programs each year and that, in state after state, include disproportionately high numbers of black schoolchildren. The system has ballooned into more than a $30 billion-a-year industry, and the costs are climbing. More troubling, nearly 40 years after *Brown v. Board of Education*, the U.S. Supreme Court's landmark school desegregation ruling, Americans continue to pay for and send their children to classrooms that are often separate and unequal.

Presented with the results of the *U.S. News* investigation, Secretary of Education Richard Riley acknowledged serious flaws in the special education system. As a result of that, Riley pledged to make fundamental reforms in the special education system in 1994. Says Riley: "The need for disabled students coming out of high school to be productive citizens is much, much greater today than in the past."

The magazine's principal findings:

• *Funding*. Special education programs often operate in ways specifically designed to attract state and federal dollars to local school districts—not to best serve students. In nearly two thirds of the 50 states, *U.S. News* found that reimbursement formulas for special education programs had an effect in determining the number and type of such programs funded. Texas, for instance, pays local school districts 10 times more for teaching special education students in separate classrooms than in classrooms with other students. The result? Despite generally accepted evidence that some special education students benefit from regular classrooms, only 5 percent of all special education students in Texas are taught in regular classrooms. That's the lowest rate in the nation. In Tennessee, thousands of special education students who had been receiving training just a few hours a week in separate classrooms were assigned to nearly all-day classes in separate rooms. The reason: a change in the state's special education funding formula that gave school districts more money to teach special education students in separate rooms.

• *Growth*. Imprecise state and federal regulations not only allow frequent misdesignation of special education students, they also drive up

> *"The [special education] system has ballooned into more than a $30 billion-a-year industry."*

the size and cost of the special education system. Since the implementation of the IDEA legislation, the number of students in special education has increased every year without exception. Today [in 1993], there are 5 million special education students in the nation's schools—10 percent of all students enrolled. One result of the system's growth: a bloated bureaucracy that even advocates of special education say is unnecessarily expensive. In Connecticut, for instance, a separate transportation system costs taxpayers 10 times more to bus a special ed student than one attending regular classes. Separate transit systems for special education students exist in most states. Some cost more than Connecticut's. Nationally, the bill for all special education services has rocketed from roughly $1 billion in 1977 to more than $30 billion in 1993.

> *"Black students are overrepresented in special education programs."*

• *Incentives.* Many principals have raised their schools' scores on statewide competency exams by placing low-scoring students in special education programs—children who might otherwise not be in special education. In most states, special education students are exempted from reading and mathematics exams; average school test scores, as a result, are higher. Such scores are important to administrators' performance and compensation reviews. Researchers Richard Allington and Anne McGill-Franzen of the State University of New York at Albany found this pattern widespread in New York. *U.S. News* documented numerous other examples.

Ambiguity and Overrepresentation

• *Classification.* Special education labels are so ambiguous that classifications vary from state to state—and even from school district to school district. Fifteen percent of all Massachusetts students wind up in special education programs, for instance. Yet in Hawaii, just 7 percent of all students are in special education; in Georgia and Michigan, only 8 percent. Classifications vary wildly from state to state, even within special education categories. In Alaska, only 3 percent of all special education students are classified as retarded; in Alabama, 28 percent.

There are not even hard and fast rules on how to define a retarded child. In Ohio, a child with an IQ level below 80 is considered mentally retarded. Move across the border to Kentucky, and the same child is placed in a regular classroom and taught along with all the other students. The anomalies are endless. Should special education students be taught in separate classrooms or regular classrooms? There are few meaningful guidelines. The result: In North Dakota, 72 percent of the state's special education students are taught in regular classrooms. In South Dakota, a state with almost identical demographics, only 8 percent of special ed students go to class with nondisabled children.

• *Race.* In 39 states, according to a *U.S. News* analysis of Department of Education data, black students are overrepresented in special education programs, compared with their percentage of the overall student population. Significantly, the analysis found that black students are most likely to be overrepresented in special education classes when they are students in predominantly *white* school districts. In some school districts, neither the number of black students nor household demographics accounted for the high percentage of black students, the *U.S. News* analysis found. Among those with the highest percentage of black special ed students not accounted for by demographics or black enrollment: South Country Central, in East Patchogue, N.Y.; Fordyce, Ark.; Compton Unified, Calif.; and Emerson, Ark. These findings tend to support arguments by critics of the special education system who attribute the overrepresentation of African-American students in the system to cultural bias in testing and placement procedures—not to any inherently high level of disability.

> *"Special education classrooms often become convenient places for teachers to send struggling students."*

• *Oversight.* Lax enforcement by state and federal agencies has allowed classification problems to persist. A *U.S. News* analysis of 10,147 discrimination complaints reviewed by the Department of Education's Office of Civil Rights since 1987 found just *one* case in which the office imposed the most severe penalty—revoking federal funds. School districts usually are allowed to work with regulators to design corrective measures. But with penalties invoked so rarely, critics say, there is little incentive for educators to address some recurrent problems.

Federal regulators often don't even know about some problems because information they receive is frequently misleading. New York State submitted data on graduation rates of special education students for a report to Congress. A *U.S. News* reporter reviewed the submission and found that it included information on just 9,418 of New York's 324,677 special education students. New York officials admit the misreporting.

• *Service.* Special education classrooms often become convenient places for teachers to send struggling students they don't want in their classrooms; academics, in such cases, takes a back seat. Indeed, special ed instructors often do as much social work—sometimes known as "life skills"—as teaching. In one special ed classroom in Ohio, students learned how to bake a frozen pizza in an oven.

Difficulties in Labeling

In theory at least, special education is simple. A child thought by his parents or teachers to have a learning problem is given a test, any problem is identified and necessary assistance is provided. Federal regulations list 13 types of disabilities that affect learning: autism, deaf-blindness, deafness, hearing impairment, mental retardation, multiple disabilities, orthopedic impairment, chronic or acute health problems (like a heart condition or epilepsy), serious emotional disturbance, specific learning disability, speech or language impairment, traumatic brain injury and visual impairment, including blindness. Only a few of these disabilities, such as deafness or blindness, can be measured by objective tests.

The rest can be highly subjective, and this is where mislabeling can occur.

Consider "learning disabilities." By far the largest class of special education students, at 49.9 percent, learning-disabled pupils are the most difficult to identify properly. One reason is definition. A learning-disabled child, according to the Department of Education, is one who has "a severe discrepancy between achievement and intellectual ability." This is squishy territory. The perceptual or processing difficulties that many think of as learning disabilities—dyslexia, for instance, in which a person reads letters in reverse order—account for just a small percentage of all learning-disabled students.

The definitional problem is compounded by another. It is up to state education departments to suggest which tests and procedures are used to measure a learning disability, and as a result, school practices can vary widely. Federal law requires that more than one test be used to identify a learning disability and that more than one individual be involved in making the determination. But such precautions are thin protection against the possibility of mislabeling a child. In fact, says University of Minnesota researcher James Ysseldyke, more than 80 percent of *all* schoolchildren in America could qualify as learning-disabled according to one or more of the various definitions now used by states.

The Role of Funding

Nothing drives the special education system like money. No state has more students classified as emotionally disturbed than Connecticut, for example. But it's not that there is more stress, paranoia or pathology there. It's simply that the state's complex funding formula encourages school districts to send emotionally disturbed students to separate schools, according to special education expert Thomas Nerney, who takes Connecticut's system to task in a report published by the Western Connecticut Association for Human Rights. Nerney notes that some cities, like New Haven, actually save money when they send students to out-of-district schools, even though these schools can cost more than $100,000 per student, because the state picks up the bulk of the cost.

> *"More than 80 percent of all schoolchildren in America could qualify as learning-disabled."*

The Constitution State is hardly alone. Twenty-three states have funding formulas that reward school districts with more tax dollars if they place more students in special ed programs. Two decades ago, when most disabled kids received little or no education, "weighted" programs made sense: The financial incentives induced school districts to start providing services to children with learning problems. Now, however, such weighted formulas often serve as money magnets. By identifying students with only minor disabilities, educators can demand more money for their schools—and get it. The trouble is, besides the financial burdens created, kids can be hurt by stigmatizing special education labels.

Labels Matter

Funding formulas also determine what kind of teachers are hired—and what kind of special education schools deliver. Contrary to national trends, for example, since the mid-1980s, Ohio has had just a tiny increase in learning-disabled students. During this same period, the state stopped providing extra money to school districts that hired instructors for children with learning disabilities.

> *"[Labels] determine how teachers choose to educate children—or whether they attempt to teach them at all."*

There are reasons for differences in special education enrollment from community to community, but because of the subjective criteria employed throughout the system, such differences are often exaggerated. In Georgia, educators classify 32 percent of the state's special education students as having learning disabilities. Rhode Island, employing different criteria, categorizes twice that many learning-disabled students, 63 percent. "Who has a disability," says Brian McNulty, Colorado's special education director, "is much more a function of *where* one lives than anything else."

And labels *do* matter. They determine how teachers choose to educate children—or whether they attempt to teach them at all. Alfred Profeet is a case in point. Struggling to read, he was forced to switch schools and ended up in a separate class for learning-disabled children. Assigned to a classroom where academic subjects were not emphasized, Alfred's basic math and reading abilities plummeted. His mother, Zipporah Profeet, saw her son's self-confidence deteriorate. She found a lawyer and a specialist who ran new tests. Alfred's real problem—he has trouble focusing his eyes—is minor and could be dealt with in a regular classroom. In November 1993, the 10-year-old was allowed to return to his old school in Queens, N.Y. His classmates greeted him with hugs at the front door. Today, Alfred is working hard to catch up academically. But his mother is bitter. Her son, she says, "lost two years out of his life."

The vagaries in the special education system can make children and parents prisoners of geography. This is what happened to the Flair family. Connie Flair wants her daughter Katie to go to her local school so she can develop ties to her community. Instead, affluent Bloomfield Hills, Mich., chooses to transport the mentally retarded 14-year-old—on a bus by herself—to an out-of-district school. If the Flairs moved 2 miles north on the street they live on now, they would be in another district, which would allow Katie to attend the local school. The same would be true if they moved 3 miles south. Connie Flair thinks this is unfair. Why, she asks, "should a family have to move?"

Racial Discrepancies

Of all problems with the nation's special education system, none is more troubling than its racial imbalance, particularly in categories like retardation.

Mental retardation can be caused by the conditions of poverty—as when a mother fails to get prenatal care or an infant chews lead paint chips. But the large number of blacks in special ed programs cannot be explained by socio-economic factors alone.

The *U.S. News* analysis found that blacks are twice as likely as whites to be classified as mentally retarded while white students are placed much more often than blacks in the less stigmatizing category of "learning-disabled." Some critics, like Harold Dent of the Center for the Study of Minorities in Special Education at Hampton University, argue that "culturally biased" IQ tests used to classify students are at least partially responsible for the disproportionate numbers of black students in special education. California seems to prove the point. Contrary to national trends, 68 percent of blacks in special education in California are classified as learning-disabled. The reason: A federal court barred the state from using IQ tests to classify black students for special education.

The role of race can be starkly clear. The Perry County and Mountain Brook school districts in Alabama have the same number of special education students. In Perry County, in the state's impoverished, cotton-farming "Black Belt," 236 students are labeled mentally retarded and 14 learning-disabled. The Mountain Brook district is farther north, a wealthy suburb of Birmingham. There, the numbers are reversed: 271 youngsters are classified as learning-disabled, only 15 as mentally retarded. Demographically, the two districts could not be more different. Perry County's residents are 96 percent black. Mountain Brook is 99 percent white.

> *"Blacks are twice as likely as whites to be classified as mentally retarded."*

In such situations, race can be a self-fulfilling prophecy. Geraldine Tubbs Moore teaches some of Perry County's mentally retarded students at West Side Middle School. She recalls vividly the advice she heard at the college where she was studying for her teaching degree: Get certified in mental retardation, she was told, because that is a black disorder. Thirteen of Perry County's 18 special education teachers are certified to teach mentally retarded children. Each year, there always seem to be enough mentally retarded students to keep them busy.

Low Expectations

In Mountain Brook, by contrast, school officials bend over backward to classify kids as learning-disabled. The label is less stigmatizing, and it typically results in the placement of students in more rigorous academic programs than if they were classified as mentally retarded. That is clear at Mountain Brook High School, where nearly every student with a learning disability takes all regular classes and 97 percent go on to college. Almost all of Mountain Brook's few children who are labeled mentally retarded have some clear genetic condition. Just three teachers are retained to teach them. "When kids are inappropriately labeled mentally retarded," says Carol Standifer, Mountain Brook's special education coordinator, "there are low expectations from those around them."

One reason for such disparities is lax enforcement by federal regulators. Although the U.S. Department of Education's Office of Civil Rights received several hundred complaints of excessive bunching of minority students in low-ability tracks in 1991, it scheduled only eight investigations. According to a critical report by the U.S. General Accounting Office, the civil rights office rarely followed up when it found evidence of violations.

> *"About 1 in 4 special education students drops out of high school."*

America's special education system today is a far cry from what Congress envisioned when it passed the pathbreaking IDEA legislation in 1975. Disabled children, the law's sponsors vowed, would be guaranteed a "free appropriate public education." Lawmakers, says Lisa Walker, a key Senate aide who helped draft the law, envisioned disabled youngsters being taught alongside other students, with additional aides and support as needed. To make that happen, IDEA promised that Washington would reimburse 40 percent of a state's costs to educate handicapped children.

That promise has proved hollow. Today, just 7 percent of a special education student's cost is repaid by Washington, and the resentment in state capitals has resulted in considerable apathy toward or hostility to special education. The U.S. Supreme Court appeared to take note of this in 1993, ruling that a South Carolina school district must reimburse the family of a learning-disabled teenager for the tuition paid to send the youngster to private school. Finding for the family, the justices agreed with lower courts that South Carolina officials had failed to educate the youngster properly.

Proposed Solutions

Today, more special educators are looking for ways to cut costs and make the system work better. There is much room for improvement. About 1 in 4 special education students drops out of high school; 43 percent of those who graduate remain unemployed three to five years after high school, and nearly one third—primarily those with learning and emotional disabilities—are arrested at least once after leaving high school.

Parents and some special educators are trying a number of solutions. Inclusion of children with learning problems in ordinary classrooms is a concept that is growing in favor. It is also one that is close to the intent of the IDEA legislation. Carlos Oberti of New Jersey says it has allowed his young son with Down's syndrome to grow socially and academically. Other parents note that it can save money on overlapping services—like the separate bus Ginger Spiers's daughter was required to take even after she transferred from a special education program in Norwalk, Conn., to a regular classroom. Yet for every parent with a story of inclusion's wonders, there is another with a cautionary tale. Some students, such as deaf children, may learn best in segregated classrooms. Inclusion also can be problematic when schools try to cut costs by placing a child with learning problems into a regular classroom without supports. The regular teacher then has to do two jobs, causing all students to suffer.

There are few other beacons of hope. New York City has a promising pilot program that is moving many children from pre-kindergarten through second grade out of special education and into mainstream classrooms. Two fifths of the children who have completed the program have been reclassified as regular students. In Vermont, a new funding formula stops rewarding school districts for putting students in special education. The result: The number of special education students in the state has dropped by 18 percent between 1990 and 1993.

Additional reason for hope comes from the changes Education Secretary Riley promises from Washington. In a 1993 interview with *U.S. News* reporters, Riley and Tom Hehir, the department's director of special education, said they plan to propose fundamental changes when Congress considers reauthorization of the IDEA law in 1994. While Riley, Hehir and Assistant Secretary Judith Heumann are committed to preserving the educational opportunities protected by the law, they intend to recommend that lawmakers:

• Make sure that children served by the special education system are truly disabled. "We are concerned," says Hehir, "about the misidentification of students and the overidentification of students."

• Encourage school systems to educate more special education students in their neighborhood schools. "Let's bring services to kids," Hehir says, "not kids to services as we do now."

• Raise academic standards in special education. Riley believes that special ed students should not be exempt from state testing programs.

• Shift federal oversight of special education away from its present emphasis on whether school systems are following bureaucratic procedures to a new emphasis on the performance of local special education efforts to end the over-representation of minorities and return children to local schools.

The reforms, if implemented, could change the lives of thousands of the nation's schoolchildren.

Mainstreaming Helps Disabled Children Adapt to Society

by Irene Culver

About the author: *Irene Culver is a freelance writer in Orangevale, California.*

The brown-eyed, auburn-haired little boy sitting next to me in a car seat as I drive to preschool asks, "Did you know my mom and dad made me?" Guardedly, I agree they did. "Shoulda used Play-Doh," he quips. His disability isn't on his mind. He's not suggesting they could have made an improved version of Carl. He's just seen a connection between making something with clay and making a baby.

Being Different

For long periods each day my grandson Carl doesn't think about his disability, but if it's brought to mind by a classmate or stranger he'll sometimes hang his head and plead, "I want to go home now."

Home is a safe place, but preschool is where he encounters the world—a world he must live in or be forever isolated. In that world, he's different. Being different often means being wrong. "What's wrong with him?" children and adults ask.

In Carl's preschool world, all the other children walk. He crawls. He can crawl around physical barriers, but the social ones sometimes block his progress.

Carl was born six weeks early. He couldn't breathe. For long frightening moments we watched through a window as he struggled for air, his chest caving in all the way to his backbone. Finally oxygen was given, but too late. He had Hyaline Membrane disease, brain damage and sleep apnea. For three weeks he hovered at the edge of death in the neonatal unit of a northern California hospi-

Irene Culver, "Why Carl Needs His Pillow," *Progressive*, September 1993. Reprinted by permission of the *Progressive*, 409 E. Main St., Madison, WI 53703.

tal, then for six months wore a heart-lung monitor. The alarm sounded many times, but he survived.

For over a year, there was no diagnosis. Floppy and lethargic, he needed twenty hours of sleep a day and cried when he didn't get it. He captivated us with his tiny curled fists and toes—signals, though we didn't know it then, of cerebral palsy. Only later were there clearer signs: his trunk was weak, his legs and arms high-toned. Then we were told: Carl has cerebral palsy.

Cerebral palsy is a catch-all term for brain damage that manifests itself in various mobility and cognition problems. Carl has spastic diplegia (stiff legs), a weak trunk, and inter-

> *"Preschool is where [Carl] encounters the world—a world he must live in or be forever isolated."*

mittently affected arms and eyes. Intellectually he is not affected.

The Americans with Disabilities Act (ADA) mandates that disabled children be placed in schools with "the least restrictive environment" they can manage. For Carl, that meant mainstream. But finding a school that would take him wasn't easy. The first school we applied to flat-out refused to make ADA-mandated changes to the playground. Carl could not negotiate the deep sand with his walker. With his stiff legs, he could not be placed in a baby swing and was too weak to swing in a regular one.

The authorities gave us reasons for not making the playground accessible: If we install a swing for him, they said, we'll soon have 500-pound adults lining up, waiting to use the baby swings; if we make changes, he may not like them by the time he is eight years old; if we make changes, he may get worse and not be able to use them. So instead of making any changes, they proposed tying Carl to the merry-go-round.

Finally realizing their legal culpability, the school officials grudgingly agreed to some small improvements. But fearing retribution against Carl, my daughter abandoned her attempt to enroll him.

The second school we applied to had fewer barriers. The playground was hard, packed dirt, more accessible than sand to a child who sometimes uses a walker and sometimes crawls. There were home-made things like a mound of dirt with a tunnel through it and a large sandbox a child could sit in. The teacher seemed ready to welcome him.

Efforts Toward Inclusion

But in spite of our show-and-tell efforts (bringing dolls with disabilities, tiny crutches, wheelchairs, stories about children with disabilities, explanation of Carl's specific disability and how it affects him), Carl is left out of many play activities. Parents plan and carry out those activities. One day, the twenty-four able-bodied children were given tin-can stilts. Carl was given nothing. Of course, children without disabilities must run and play and walk. But activities that include the only child with a disability could also be planned.

We go to school with Carl every day to help him move from one activity to another, to place him in his special cube-chair at the table, and on his block at circle time. When the other children dance, we hold him under his arms and help him dance, too. But all the efforts toward inclusion are our efforts, not the teacher's or the other parents'.

Often the children play that Carl is their baby; other times they ignore him. But once I saw him joyfully wrestling with his favorite friends. Another time he played with a toy service station and cars and trucks, and soon other children joined him. They were all equal: playing on the floor, crawling around pushing little cars. Not walking was irrelevant.

But he gets tired, and sometimes sleeps through most of the preschool day, curled up on a little couch in the dollhouse. Sometimes his feelings are hurt. One day a little boy mocked him, using his walker, grimacing, throwing his body forward awkwardly, calling out, "I'm Carl!"

> *"We're doing all we can to make any dream Carl may have come true."*

Educators, other parents, grandparents, therapists, physicians, friends—all advise us to send Carl to a school for disabled children, with children "like himself." But those children are not like him either; most are severely retarded, while he is above age level in all intellectual areas measured. We're told that we ask too much of him. We are asking a lot. It is hard for him. But this is the real world and he will live in the real world all his life.

Carl has become strong since he started preschool. Before, a few minutes using his walker exhausted him. Now he can explore all the aisles of the local toystore. He loves to play with his classmates, even if he has to be the baby. Sometimes during circle-time, he crawls to the teacher and, with our help, stands up to show-and-tell, just like the other children do. One day, standing there with support, he asked the other children. "Do you know where my dreams are?" Receiving no answer, he triumphantly told them, "They're in my pillow!"

His dreams are in his pillow—that's why he carries it wherever he goes. We're doing all we can to make any dream Carl may have come true. The ADA gives us that right.

Deaf Children Can Benefit from Mainstreaming

by Edward Dolnick

About the author: *Edward Dolnick is a contributing editor of* Health *magazine.*

For millennia deafness was considered so catastrophic that very few ventured to ease its burdens. Isolation in a kind of permanent solitary confinement was deemed inevitable; a deaf person, even in the midst of urban hubbub, was considered as unreachable as a fairy-tale princess locked in a tower. The first attempts to educate deaf children came only in the sixteenth century. As late as 1749 the French Academy of Sciences appointed a commission to determine whether deaf people were "capable of reasoning." Today no one would presume to ignore the deaf or exclude them from full participation in society. But acknowledging their rights is one thing, coming to grips with their plight another. Deafness is still seen as a dreadful fate.

Disability or Subculture?

Lately, though, the deaf community has begun to speak for itself. To the surprise and bewilderment of outsiders, its message is utterly contrary to the wisdom of centuries: Deaf people, far from groaning under a heavy yoke, are not handicapped at all. Deafness is not a disability. Instead, many deaf people now proclaim, they are a subculture like any other. They are simply a linguistic minority (speaking American Sign Language) and are no more in need of a cure for their condition than are Haitians or Hispanics.

That view is vehemently held. "The term 'disabled' describes those who are blind or physically handicapped," the deaf linguists Carol Padden and Tom Humphries write, "not Deaf people." (The upper-case D is significant: it serves as a succinct proclamation that the deaf share a culture rather than merely a medical condition.) So strong is the feeling of cultural solidarity that many deaf parents cheer on discovering that their baby is deaf. Pondering such a scene, a hearing person can experience a kind of vertigo. The surprise is not simply the

From Edward Dolnick, "Deafness as Culture," *Atlantic Monthly*, September 1993. Reprinted with permission.

unfamiliarity of the views; it is that, as in a surrealist painting, jarring notions are presented as if they were commonplaces.

The embrace of what looks indisputably like hardship is what, in particular, strikes the hearing world as perverse, and deaf leaders have learned to brace themselves for the inevitable question. "No!" Roslyn Rosen says, by shaking her head vehemently, she *wouldn't* prefer to be able to hear. Rosen, the president of the National Association of the Deaf, is deaf, the daughter of deaf parents, and the mother of deaf children. "I'm happy with who I am," she says through an interpreter, "and

> *"The crucial issue is that hearing parent and deaf child don't share a means of communication."*

I don't want to be 'fixed.' Would an Italian-American rather be a WASP? In our society everyone agrees that whites have an easier time than blacks. But do you think a black person would undergo operations to become white?"

The view that deafness is akin to ethnicity is far from unanimously held. "The world of deafness often seems Balkanized, with a warlord ruling every mountaintop," writes Henry Kisor, the book editor for the *Chicago Sun-Times* and deaf himself. But the "deaf culture" camp—Kisor calls it the "New Orthodoxy"—is in the ascendancy, and its proponents invoke watchwords that still carry echoes of earlier civil-rights struggles. "Pride," "heritage," "identity," and similar words are thick in the air.

Rhetoric aside, however, the current controversy is disorientingly unfamiliar, because the deaf are a group unlike any ethnic minority: 90 percent of all deaf children are born to hearing parents. Many people never meet a deaf person unless one is born to them. Then parent and child belong to different cultures, as they would in an adoption across racial lines. And deaf children acquire a sense of cultural identity from their peers rather than their parents, as homosexuals do. But the crucial issue is that hearing parent and deaf child don't share a means of communication. Deaf children cannot grasp their parents' spoken language, and hearing parents are unlikely to know sign language. Communication is not a gift automatically bestowed in infancy but an acquisition gained only by laborious effort. . . .

The Challenge of Lip-Reading

Because antibiotics have tamed many of the childhood diseases that once caused permanent loss of hearing, more than 90 percent of all deaf children in the United States today were born deaf or lost their hearing before they had learned English. The challenge that faces them—recognizing that other peoples' mysterious lip movements *are* language, and then learning to speak that language—is immeasurably greater than that facing an adult who must cope with a gradual hearing loss.

Learning to speak is so hard for people deaf from infancy because they are trying, without any direct feedback, to mimic sounds they have never heard. (Children who learn to speak and then go deaf fare better, because they retain some memory of sound.) One mother of a deaf child describes the challenge as comparable to learning to speak Japanese from within a soundproof glass booth. And even if a deaf person does learn to speak, understanding someone else's speech remains maddeningly difficult. Countless words look alike on the lips, though they sound quite different. "Mama" is indistinguishable from "papa," "cat" from "hat," "no new taxes" from "go to Texas." Context and guesswork are crucial, and conversation becomes a kind of fast and ongoing crossword puzzle.

"Speechreading is EXHAUSTING. I hate having to depend on it," writes Cheryl Heppner, a deaf woman who is the executive director of the Northern Virginia Resource Center for Deaf and Hard of Hearing Persons. Despite her complaint, Heppner is a speech-reading virtuoso. She made it through public school and Pennsylvania State University without the help of interpreters, and she says she has never met a person with better speech-reading skills. But "even with peak conditions," she explains, "good lighting, high energy level, and a person who articulates well, I'm still guessing at half of what I see on the lips.". . .

For the average deaf person, lip-reading is even less rewarding. In tests using simple sentences, deaf people recognize perhaps three or four words in every ten. Ironically, the greatest aid to lip-reading is knowing how words sound. One British study found, for example, that the average deaf person with a decade of practice was no better at lip-reading than a hearing person picked off the street.

> *"The average deaf sixteen-year-old reads at the level of a hearing eight-year-old."*

Unsurprisingly, the deaf score poorly on tests of English skills. The average deaf sixteen-year-old reads at the level of a hearing eight-year-old. When deaf students eventually leave school, three in four are unable to read a newspaper. Only two deaf children in a hundred (compared with forty in a hundred among the general population) go on to college. Many deaf students write English as if it were a foreign language. . . .

American Sign Language

Small wonder that many of the deaf eagerly turn to American Sign Language, invariably described as "the natural language of the deaf." Deaf children of deaf parents learn ASL as easily as hearing children learn a spoken language. At the same age that hearing babies begin talking, deaf babies of parents who sign begin "babbling" nonsense signs with their fingers. Soon, and without having to be formally taught, they have command of a rich and varied language, as expressive as English but as different from it as Urdu or Hungarian.

At the heart of the idea that deafness is cultural, in fact, is the deaf community's proprietary pride in ASL. . . .

ASL is the everyday language of perhaps half a million Americans. A shared language makes for a shared identity. With the deaf as with other groups, this identity is a prickly combination of pride in one's own ways and wariness of outsiders. "If I happened to strike up a relationship with a hearing person," says MJ Bienvenu, a deaf activist speaking through an interpreter, "I'd have considerable trepidation about my [deaf] parents' reaction. They'd ask, 'What's the matter? Aren't your own people good enough for you?' and they'd warn, 'They'll take advantage of you. You don't know what they're going to do behind your back.'"

> *"Many profoundly deaf adults participate fully and successfully in the hearing world."*

Blind men and women often marry sighted people, but 90 percent of deaf people who marry take deaf spouses. When social scientists ask people who are blind or in wheelchairs if they wish they could see or walk, they say yes instantly. Only the deaf answer the equivalent question no. The essence of deafness, they explain, is not the lack of hearing but the community and culture based on ASL. Deaf culture represents not a denial but an affirmation.

Spokespeople for deaf pride present their case as self-evident and commonsensical. Why should anyone expect deaf people to deny their roots when every other cultural group proudly celebrates its traditions and history? Why stigmatize the speakers of a particular language as disabled? "When Gorbachev visited the U.S., he used an interpreter to talk to the President," says Bienvenu, who is one of the directors of an organization called The Bicultural Center. "Was Gorbachev disabled?". . .

Objections to Mainstreaming

Historically, advocates for every disabled group have directed their fiercest fire at policies that exclude their group. No matter the good intentions, no matter the logistical hurdles, they have insisted, separate is not equal. Thus buildings, buses, classes, must be accessible to all; special accommodations for the disabled are not a satisfactory substitute. All this has become part of conventional wisdom. Today, under the general heading of "mainstreaming," it is enshrined in law and unchallenged as a premise of enlightened thought.

Except among the deaf. Their objection is that even well-meaning attempts to integrate deaf people into hearing society may actually imprison them in a zone of silence. Jostled by a crowd but unable to communicate, they are effectively alone. The problem is especially acute in schools, where mainstreaming has led to the decline of residential schools for the disabled and the deaf and the integration of many such students into ordinary public schools. Since deafness is rare, affecting one child in a thousand, deaf students are thinly scattered. As a result, half of all deaf children in public school have either no deaf classmates at all or very few.

"Mainstreaming deaf children in regular public-school programs," the prominent deaf educator Leo Jacobs writes, will produce "a new generation of educational failures" and "frustrated and unfulfilled adults." Another deaf spokesman, Mervin Garretson, is even harsher. The danger of mainstreaming, he contends, is that deaf children could be "educationally, vocationally, and emotionally mutilated."

In his brilliant and polemical book *The Mask of Benevolence*, Harlan Lane, the chief theoretician of the deaf-culture movement, makes his case seem as clear-cut as a proposition in formal logic. Deaf children are biologically equipped to do everything but hear, he argues; spoken language turns on the ability to hear; therefore spoken language is a poor choice for deaf children. For good measure, Lane throws in a corollary: Since an alternative language, ASL, is both available and easy for the deaf to learn, ASL is a better choice for a first language.

For the parents of a deaf child, though, matters are far from simple. (Lane is childless.) Parents have crucial decisions to make, and they don't have the luxury of time. Children who learn a language late are at a lifelong disadvantage. Deafness is, in one scholar's summary, "a curable, or rather a preventable, form of mental retardation."

Osmond and Deborah Crosby's daughter was born in July of 1988. "Dorothy Jane Crosby," the birth announcement began, "Stanford class of 2009, track, academic all-American, B.S. in pre-astronautics, Cum Laude. 2008 Olympics (decathlon), Miss Florida, Senate hopeful."

"You can chuckle about that announcement," Oz Crosby says now, "but we all have expectations for our kids. That card was a message from my unconscious—these are the kinds of things I'd like to see, that would make me proud, in my child. And the first thing that happened after DJ's deafness was diagnosed was that I felt that child had died. That's something you hear a lot from parents, and it's that blunt and that real."

> *"Since spoken language is the ticket to the larger world, isn't giving a child ASL as a first language a bit risky?"*

Crosby, fifty, is tall and athletic, with blond hair and a small, neat moustache. A timber executive who now lives in the suburbs of Washington, D.C., he is a serious and intelligent man who had scarcely given deafness a thought before it invaded his household. Then he plunged into the deafness literature and began keeping a journal of his own.

Communication Problems

He found that every path was pocked with hazards. The course that sounds simplest, keeping the child at home with her parents and teaching her English, can prove fantastically difficult. Even basic communication is a constant challenge. In a memoir called *Deaf Like Me*, a man named Thomas Spradley tells of raising a deaf daughter, Lynn. One Saturday morning shortly after Lynn had begun school, Spradley and his wife, Louise, found her outdoors, waiting for the school bus. Lynn stood at the end of the driveway, scanning the street every few seconds. After half an hour she gave up and came indoors. For weeks Lynn repeated the same futile wait every Saturday and Sunday, until her parents finally managed to convey the concept of "weekday" and "weekend." Words like "car" and "shoes" were easy; abstractions and relationships were not. The Spradleys knew Lynn loved her grandparents, for instance, but they had no idea if she knew who those devoted elderly people were. When Lynn once had to undergo a spinal tap, her parents could not explain what the painful test was for.

> *"Cued speech is, essentially, English."*

As much trouble as Thomas and Louise Spradley had in talking with their daughter, she was just as frustrated in trying to communicate with them. "How do you tell Mommy that you don't like your cereal with that much milk on it?" Spradley writes. "How do you ask Daddy to swing you upside down when all he seems to understand is that you want to be held? How do you tell them that you want to go to other people's houses like [her older brother]? How do you make them understand you want the same kind of Kool-Aid that you had two weeks ago at your cousin's house and just now remembered? How do you say, 'I forgot what I wanted'?"

Making matters more frustrating still, no one seems able to tell parents how successful their child will be in speaking and understanding English. "I'd ask, 'What's the future for us?'" Crosby says, "and they'd say, 'Every deaf child is different.'" Though given to measured, even pedantic, phrasing, Crosby grows angry as he recalls the scene. "It seemed like such a cop-out. I wanted to grab them by the throat and shout, 'Here's the bloody audiogram. How's she going to talk?'"

The truth, Crosby has reluctantly come to concede, is that only a few generalizations are possible. Children who are born deaf or who lose their hearing before learning to speak have a far harder time than those deafened later. Children with a profound hearing loss have a harder time than children with a mild loss. Children who cannot detect high-pitched sounds have problems different from those of children who cannot detect low pitches. Finally, and unaccountably, some deaf children just happen to have an easier time with spoken English than others.

Hence few overall statistics are available. Those few are not encouraging. In one study, for example, teachers of the deaf, evaluating their own pupils, judged the speech of two thirds of them to be hard to understand or unintelligible. Timothy Jaech, the superintendent of the Wisconsin School for the Deaf, writes, "The vast majority of deaf children will never develop intelligible speech for the general public." Jaech, who is deaf, speaks and reads lips. "To gamble 12 to 15 years of a deaf child's life is almost immoral," he says. "[My sister] and I were among the lucky ones. What of the other 99 percent?"

Difficult Decisions

Still, it is indisputable that many profoundly deaf adults participate fully and successfully in the hearing world, as lawyers and engineers and in dozens of other roles. Do these examples show what parents might expect for their own child? Or are they inspiring but irrelevant tales that have as little bearing on the typical deaf child as Michael Jordan's success has on the future of a ten-year-old dreaming of NBA glory?

The case for ASL has problems of its own. ASL is certainly easier for the deaf child to learn, but what of the rest of the family? How can parents say anything meaningful to their child in a foreign language they have only begun to study? Moreover, many hearing parents point out, even if deaf culture is rich and vital, it is indisputably not the majority culture. Since spoken language is the ticket to the larger world, isn't giving a child ASL as a first language a bit risky?

The choices are agonizing. "I understand now how people choosing a cancer therapy for their child must feel," Crosby says. "You can't afford to be wrong." To illustrate the dilemma, Crosby wrote what he calls a parable:

> Suppose that your one-year-old, who has been slow to walk, has just been diagnosed with a rare disorder of the nervous system. The prognosis is for great difficulty in muscular control of the arms and legs due to tremors and impaired nerve pathways. With the help of special braces, physical therapy, and lots of training, she will be able to walk slowly, climb stairs haltingly, and use her hands awkwardly. In general, she will be able to do most of the things other kids do, although not as easily, smoothly, or quickly. Some children respond to this therapy better than others, but all can get around on their legs after a fashion. Even though they will never run or play sports, they will have complete mobility at a deliberate, shuffling pace.

> There *is* an alternative, however. If her legs are amputated right away, the tremors will cease, and the remaining nerve pathways will strengthen. She will be able to use a wheelchair with ease. She can even be a wheelchair athlete, "running" marathons, playing basketball, etc., if she desires. Anywhere a wheelchair can go is readily available to her. There is easy access to a world that is geographically smaller. On the other hand, she can't climb simple stairs, hike trails slowly, or even use public transportation without special assistance.

"Now, Mr. and Mrs. Solomon," Crosby concluded, "which life do *you* choose for your child?"

Cued Speech

Crosby and his wife have chosen a compromise, a controversial technique called cued speech, in which spoken English is accompanied by hand signals that enable a deaf person to distinguish between words that look alike on the lips. The aim is to remove the guesswork from lip-reading by using eight hand shapes in different positions near the face to indicate that the word being spoken is, say, "bat" rather than "pan."

The technique, which is spread by a tiny but zealous group of parents with deaf children, has several advantages. It's easy to learn, for one thing, taking only twenty or so hours of study. A parent who sets out to learn American Sign Language, in contrast, must devote months or years to the project, as he would have to do in order to learn any foreign language. And since cued speech is, essentially, English, parents can bypass the stilted, often useless phrases of the beginning language student. Instead of stumbling over "*la plume de ma tante*," they can talk to their deaf child from the beginning about any subject in the world.

> "*A deaf child who learns cued speech learns English . . . as his native language.*"

Moreover, because cued speech is simply English transliterated, rather than a new language, nothing has to be lost in translation. A deaf child who learns cued speech learns English, along with its slang and jargon and idioms and jokes, as his native language. "It's a way to embrace English, the language your whole country runs on, instead of trying to pretend it doesn't exist," says Judy Weiss, a woman in Washington, D.C., who has used cued speech with her son since he lost his hearing as a ten-month-old.

This method, which was invented at Gallaudet in 1965–1966, is nonetheless out of favor with the deaf community. It's seen as a slap at ASL and as just a new version of the despised "oralism," in which deaf students were forced for hour upon hour to try to pronounce English words they had never heard. But the proponents of cued speech insist that these objections are political and unfounded. They point to a handful of small studies that conclude that deaf children who learn cued speech read as well as hearing students, and they mention a small group of highly successful deaf students who rely on cuing. Perhaps the most accomplished of all is a Wellesley undergraduate named Stasie Jones. Raised in France by an American mother and a British father, she speaks French and English and is now studying Russian and Spanish.

But the system is no godsend. "The trap I see a lot of cuing families fall into," Crosby says, "is to say, 'Johnny understands everything we say, we understand everything he says, he's getting *A*s at school—what's the problem?' The problem is, Johnny can't talk to someone he meets on the street and Johnny can't order a hamburger at McDonald's."

Total Communication

Cued speech is used only in a relative handful of schools. By far the most common method of teaching the deaf today is called "total communication." The idea is that teachers use any and all means of communication with their students—speech, writing, ASL, finger-spelling. Total communication was instituted in the 1970s as a reaction to a century of oralism, in which signing was forbidden and the aim was to teach the deaf child to speak and lip-read.

Oralism still has zealous adherents, but today it is used mainly with hard-of-hearing students and only rarely with deaf ones. Its dominance began with the Congress of Milan, an international meeting of educators in 1880, which affirmed "the incontestable superiority of speech over sign" and voted to banish sign language from deaf education. The ban, notorious to this day among the deaf, was effective. In 1867 every American school for the deaf taught in ASL; by 1907 not a single one did.

When total communication came along, the two rival camps in deaf education accepted it warily. Those who favored English reasoned that at least teachers would be speaking to their students; those who preferred ASL were pleased that teachers would be signing. Today hardly anyone is pleased, and one of the few points of agreement in the present debate is that deaf education is distressingly bad. The Commission on Education of the Deaf, for example, which reported to the President and Congress in 1988, began its account, "The present status of education for persons who are deaf in the United States is unsatisfactory. Unacceptably so. This is [our] primary and inescapable conclusion."

The explanation for these dreary findings, depending on who is carrying out the analysis, is either that deafness is so debilitating that poor results are inevitable or that something is wrong with current teaching methods. Total communication, its critics contend, is unworkable. No teacher can speak in English and simultaneously sign the same message in ASL, which has a completely different grammar and word order. "In practice," Harlan Lane writes, " 'total communication' merely means that the teacher may accompany his spoken English with some signs from American Sign Language, if he knows a few. While the teacher is speaking, he occasionally 'shouts' a sign—that is, signs a prominent noun or verb if he knows it, in the wrong order and without using the complex grammar of ASL."

> *"The present status of education for persons who are deaf in the United States is unsatisfactory."*

Lane and his allies support an approach called bilingual-bicultural. In this new and still rare program (so new that few measures of its success or failure are available) students are taught in ASL and eventually build on that knowledge to learn English as a second language. Since learning to speak is so difficult and time-consuming, the emphasis in English courses is on reading and writing rather than on speaking.

Neither this new approach nor any other single method may prove right for everyone. Take Cheryl Heppner, the director of the Northern Virginia Resource Center. She was deafened by meningitis as a second-grader, long after she had become expert in English. Today Heppner is a great admirer of ASL, which she learned as an adult, but she says nonetheless that classes taught in ASL would not have been best for her. "Why should they have stripped English away from me?" she asks. "I already had to learn to cope with deafness."

The objections of many hearing parents to the bilingual scheme are far more strenuous. ASL is not simply a different language, they note, but a language without a written form. Partly as a consequence, deaf culture has a marked anti-book bias. (Lane himself confesses that he is "really frustrated" that so few deaf people have read his eloquent but lengthy accounts of deaf culture.) "If you give your child, as a first language, a language that has no written form," Oz Crosby says, "and if that language on average does not lead to good reading skills, then you're giving that child a life in which she reads at a third- to fifth-grade level. She will be in danger of being exploited, because low-end jobs are all that will be available to her."

Mainstreaming Is Not Effective

by Thomas J. Murphy

About the author: *An attorney from Marlton, New Jersey, Thomas J. Murphy represented the school board in the case of* Oberti v. Clementon Board of Education, *in which full inclusion was upheld.*

Rachel, a mentally retarded, speech-impaired 9-year-old with an IQ of 44 and a mental age of 4, sits in a California classroom, obliviously staring at a textbook that is upside-down in front of her. Across the country in New Jersey, Rafael, a mentally retarded 5-year-old with an IQ of 59 and a mental age of 2 who cannot speak intelligibly and who must be taken to the bathroom every 15 minutes, creates havoc with frequent outbursts, tantrums, and assaults on teachers, aides, and other students.

The "Full Inclusion" Movement

These scenes are the result of a movement called "full inclusion," whose supporters declare that putting children like Rachel and Rafael into separate classes is a form of illegal discrimination. Proponents argue that full inclusion is required by the Individuals with Disabilities Education Act (IDEA), which says disabled children should be educated with non-disabled children "to the maximum extent appropriate." Yet IDEA also requires that public schools provide highly specialized education "designed to meet the unique needs" of handicapped children. That is precisely what full inclusion fails to do.

Backed by ideologues in the U.S. Department of Education's Office of Civil Rights, full inclusion is the latest egalitarian fad to be imposed upon the nation's schools. The purpose is to eliminate the separate education of nearly all handicapped children and force them into regular classrooms, ignoring the objections of their parents and the recommendations of professional educators. In short, it represents a triumph of liberal ideology over education under the guise of civil rights.

In its most mindless form, full inclusion puts mentally retarded, speech-impaired, non-toilet-trained, extremely disruptive children with disparate needs in regular public-school classes. These children are supposed to pursue individualized curricula with aides, under the aegis of the teacher who is attempting to teach the whole class. To accomplish this formidable task, the teacher would be expected to bone up on special education and rely on an array of consultants.

In practice, the handicapped children would be denied the small-group, multi-sensory, carefully sequenced instruction, integrated with their various physical therapies, now provided by skilled certified teachers. The non-handicapped children would be denied *their* regular instruction and, to a greater or lesser extent, see their classes converted into special-education classes. This is an educational nightmare in which all the children emerge as losers.

Teachers' Objections

"It gets complex when you have kids with a broad range of abilities," Mary Crampton, a teacher in Eden Prairie, Minnesota, told the *Wall Street Journal*. Miss Crampton had taught a seventh-grade social-studies class that included eight low-IQ children and a deaf child with cerebral palsy as well as several gifted students. She described the class as "a three-ring circus."

The American Federation of Teachers was so alarmed at the concept of full inclusion that it called for a moratorium on the practice in a December 1993 statement. "It's not just teachers who are paying the price," the AFT warned. "Inappropriate inclusion lowers expectations that any student in that classroom can get the education they deserve, and the student who needs the most help invariably suffers the most. As inclusion is increasingly practiced, it bears no resemblance to what most well-wishing people think of as mainstreaming children with disabilities into regular classrooms. It places children who cannot function into an environment which doesn't help them and often detracts from the education process for all students."

> *"Full inclusion puts mentally retarded, speech-impaired, non-toilet-trained, extremely disruptive children . . . in regular public-school classes."*

The policy presumes that handicapped children benefit by being placed with non-handicapped children. There is no scientific basis for this belief. Indeed, experience shows that such children are more isolated in the regular class, which imposes greater psychological pressure on them, resulting in behavior problems. Advocates of full inclusion respond to requests for substantiation of their claims by accusing critics of lacking sympathy for handicapped children.

Despite the dearth of evidence that full inclusion works, the policy has been endorsed by two federal appeals courts. In the 1993 case *Oberti v. Clementon Board of Education*, the U.S. Court of Appeals for the Third Circuit ruled that the school district had violated IDEA by placing Rafael Oberti in a separate special-education class. The court decided that Rafael could be satisfactorily educated in a regular classroom, despite his inability to communicate, his disruptive behavior, and his need for frequent trips to the bathroom. In the 1994 case *Holland v. Unified School District of Sacramento*, the U.S. Court of Appeals for the Ninth Circuit ruled that Rachel Holland, staring at her upside-down textbook, was a fully participating member of the class.

"Inappropriate inclusion lowers expectations that any student in that classroom can get the education they deserve."

Cases of this sort were anticipated by the U.S. Supreme Court as early as 1982. In *Hendrick Hudson Central School District v. Rowley*, Chief Justice William Rehnquist specifically warned against judicial interference with the formulation of educational methodology under IDEA: "Courts must be careful to avoid imposing their view of preferable educational methods upon the States. The primary responsibility for formulating the education to be accorded to a handicapped child, and for choosing the educational method most suitable to the child's needs, was left by the Act to State and local educational agencies."

Good and Bad News

The good news is that the cases decided in favor of full inclusion are law in only 2 of the nation's 11 federal circuits, and there is contrary case law in other circuits. The bad news is that the administrative bureaucracy that controls public schools in this country, striving to comply with guidelines from the Education Department's Office of Civil Rights and avoid lawsuits, sees these cases as the wave of the future. Whittier High School in Whittier, California, recently adopted a plan to integrate all children into regular classes, regardless of disability. Fred Zimmerman, Whittier's principal, told the *Wall Street Journal*, "With recent court cases, this will be the direction of all schools."

Suppose you are the parent of a non-handicapped child forced to attend quasi-special-education classes. Or suppose you are the parent of a handicapped child and want the special education to which your child is entitled by law. What recourse do you have? Congress can't help you, because there is nothing wrong with the law; it has simply been misinterpreted. Federal judges are not subject to the electoral process. The Supreme Court can't review *Oberti* because the school district did not appeal; it may review *Holland*, but that case does not present all the relevant issues. The Office of Civil Rights has the immunity of an entrenched federal bureaucracy.

It may take parents some time to learn what is happening to their public schools and that they are powerless to do anything about it. Once they wake up, they may choose to wait through a few years of chaos until the same federal courts tell them that the decision in *Oberti* was a mistake, that parallel instruction and full inclusion really are not mandated.

On the other hand, with the havoc of full inclusion added to gross inefficiency, court-ordered secularization, and the conversion of schools into laboratories for social experimentation, these parents may finally give up on public education and join the growing number of Americans who support school vouchers.

As the exodus from public schools continues, the public-school system could be downsized to accommodate the children of the liberals who support full inclusion—unless, of course, they are already sending their kids to private schools.

Disabled Students Disrupt Classrooms

by Stephen Goode

About the author: *Stephen Goode is a writer for* Insight, *a weekly news-magazine.*

A disabled, violent student in North Carolina broke her teacher's arm in a classroom fray. A disabled Oklahoma student stabbed her teacher with a nail she had secreted into class. What followed? Summary expulsion, or at least placement in more restrictive classrooms?

No. Under the 1975 Individuals With Disabilities Education Act, or IDEA, which provides the special programs designed to educate and create opportunities for disabled students, the teachers and school officials in the two states may deal with such violent and disruptive students with only mild punishments.

Mild Punishment for Disruptive Behavior

The Oklahoma student received a three-day suspension, for example, and the North Carolina girl was suspended from school for two days even though similar acts by nondisabled students would have resulted in much harsher measures.

Such incidents, now commonplace, have led the two major teachers' unions—the American Federation of Teachers and the National Education Association—along with several professional organizations, such as the National Association of Elementary School Principals, to demand a major overhaul of the IDEA. They believe its provisions have been responsible for allowing the situation to get completely out of hand and they are glad it is before Congress for reevaluation.

Violent and disruptive behavior by disabled students has ranged from defecating in the classroom to the regular battering of teachers and even the murder of other students.

Says Michael Resnick, spokesman for the National School Boards Association, "What we are asking is that disabled students be treated the same way as nondisabled students—that all students be viewed as equal." Resnick and other professionals want to see the IDEA revamped to protect teachers and students from violence in the classroom—allowing school authorities to remove disruptive students and, preferably, transfer them to settings in which their special needs can be met. "Nondisabled students have rights too," says Resnick.

Pitted against these educators are parents of disabled students and leaders of organizations that represent the disabled, such as the Berkeley-based Disability Rights Education and Defense Fund. These groups regard any changes in the IDEA as a slippery slope down which hard-won rights for the disabled will slide into Dickensian misery.

What special-education advocates want is a school system "where no child is deprived of education and there is no one who is expelled," says Myrna Mandlawitz, a specialist in government affairs for the national Association of State Directors of Special Education, based in Alexandria, Va. Mandlawitz argues that a strong federal presence in special education—and a strong IDEA—is needed because the states have "a bad record," particularly before the 1975 passage of this law.

The Theory Behind Inclusion

At issue is a practice called "inclusion," initiated about 15 years ago [1980] and now widespread, in which disabled students are taken from special-education centers and other specialized schools and grouped in regular classrooms with the nondisabled. The theory behind inclusion is that the disabled will benefit from association with other students and will not tend to regard themselves as irredeemably different.

According to Department of Education figures, 4.8 million school-age children are defined as disabled, the vast majority (3.5 million) of whom fall into such broad categories as the learning disabled and those with speech and language impairments—groupings that include dyslexics and the hyperactive. About 550,000 are mentally retarded, while deaf and blind students number just under 100,000.

Inclusion means mainstreaming such disabled students as dyslexics—many of whom can profit from contact with nondyslexics and only some of whom need highly individualized education, according to Steve Laubacher, executive director of the Orton Dyslexia Society, based in Baltimore.

> *"Teachers and school officials can suspend disabled students . . . for only 10 days."*

But also mainstreamed are the disabled children with Down syndrome and the autistic, who require a great deal of personal attention, who sometimes are not toilet trained (requiring schools to provide special diapering rooms) and who can be violent.

Under an IDEA "stay-put provision," teachers and school officials can suspend disabled students from any category for only 10 days without then going to court to obtain permission from a judge to continue the suspension.

It's at this point that school authorities feel most frustrated—and it is at this point that many educators who otherwise support special education become doubtful. Says John Brennan, a retired adjustment counselor in psychological services with the Boston public schools, "I think there is a need for the programs, but without the far-out social theories in which the special-ed people begin to pursue one crazy fad after another."

> *"Many states [are] fearful of a rise in the number of lawsuits from nondisabled students harmed in classrooms by the disabled."*

Going to court to remove a student deemed disruptive and a danger to him or herself and others takes time and a great deal of money. Judges are prone to grant suspension of violent students only in cases in which a life is threatened—something teachers and school officials find difficult to prove.

Moreover, the courts rarely are friendly to teachers' concerns. Their predominant philosophy is that a disability saps self-esteem—and it is this loss of confidence that leads the disabled student to lash out and turn to violence. It is an approach to the law that allows the courts to conclude that disabled students should not be punished in the same ways as nondisabled students, educators say.

In addition, the schools often end up paying their opponents' attorneys' fees. Fee awards as high as $10,000 and $20,000 are not unusual, says Resnick. These funds must come out of school budgets (and therefore from taxpayer money) and be taken from the costs of other projects the schools have planned. . . .

Proposals for Change

Educators such as Resnick, as well as advocates for the disabled, are asking the federal government to provide as much as another 40 percent of what the states are paying for special-education programs. No one in Congress is even talking about spending that kind of money. Since the states now spend about $30 billion, that would mean at least $13 billion coming from federal funds. But the federal government supplies "only" about $3 billion a year—a figure that may increase slightly . . . but which certainly won't climb by much and may go down.

The Clinton administration has checked in with a revised IDEA that would base federal grants to the states on the total number of students enrolled in school, rather than the number of special-education kids, as now is the case.

The Education Department sees this bill as encouraging the states to start identifying disabled youngsters early on—say, at the toddler stage—when disabilities, especially many kinds of learning and speech problems, are best handled.

But, more to the point, Education hopes that by basing grants on total numbers of students the states won't tend to "overidentify" children who have disabilities—a problem many observers say adds significantly to the lists of students in special education and one that needs addressing.

The administration bill doesn't address the clear and present danger of violence in the classroom, Resnick notes, and he also says that Congress has yet to deal with that problem.

What the teachers' unions and education associations want is a system that allows disputes between teachers and the representatives of the disabled to be settled in hearings outside the courtroom—with no attorneys present, says Resnick. The courts, they say, must be a last resort. It's a demand that the disabled and their representatives fight tooth and nail. All three House hearings on the bill in the summer of 1995 were heavily attended by parents of the disabled, who also staged a 1,000-person demonstration on the steps of the Capitol in favor of keeping the restrictive provisions.

The IDEA as it now stands also requires schools to pay for the hearing aids, eyeglasses and other needs of their disabled students, a cost educators want placed on state health agencies rather than the educational system, says Resnick.

Protecting Against Violence

Congress may find some way to grant teachers and others in the classroom more protection—at least when it comes to school violence. In 1994 a bill that allows schools to suspend for 45 days disabled students who bring firearms to class was supported by the Clinton administration and passed by the House and Senate. This was a major alteration in the IDEA, and it comes despite protests from advocates for the disabled. School officials say they want the 45-day suspension extended to disabled students who bring to school other weapons, such as knives, brass knuckles and martial-arts gear. Many states, some of them fearful of a rise in the number of lawsuits from nondisabled students harmed in classrooms by the disabled, are taking matters into their own hands. Virginia authorities, for example, asked a federal court to overturn a July 3, 1995, ruling by Secretary of Education Richard Riley that the commonwealth violates the IDEA when it suspends violent students who threaten others in the classroom.

Whatever happens, Boston's John Brennan may have the last word on the bottom-line issue at hand. "When kids are disruptive, you remove them," he says. "You give the other kids a break."

Disabled and Chronically Ill Students Benefit from Homeschooling

by Leese Griffith

About the author: *Leese Griffith is a contributor to the bimonthly* Home Education Magazine.

Tanya appears to be the picture of health as she romps with a visitor's child in the backyard. She's small, perhaps, and her coloring is fair, but her violet blue eyes dance with mischief and energy. This is a good day for Tanya, and her mother watches from the kitchen window, nervously.

"It's good to see her running and playing," Karen says, "but I'm always afraid she's going to over do it."

Children with Special Needs

Tanya has asthma. She's been in and out of hospitals during much of her seven years. Karen and Tom enrolled her at the neighborhood elementary school in 1993, but recurrent problems with the asthma caused her to miss more than four weeks of school during her kindergarten year. The school told Karen that they'd have to hold Tanya back, since she hadn't fulfilled the minimum attendance requirement. Frustrated and upset, Karen and Tom brought Tanya home.

Stuart's parents have struggled with a multitude of issues since he was diagnosed with a rare form of lymphoma in 1993. Their world has grown very, very small. Daily life now consists of medications, blood tests, hospital visits and sifting through an insurmountable stack of bills. If not for homeschooling, Stuart would lack the opportunity to keep up with the academic progress of his peers.

"Our schedule is so overwhelmed with his medical care," Mary says, "that we've integrated it into his homeschooling—if you could call it homeschooling."

Leese Griffith, "The Chronically Ill or Disabled 'Student,'" *Home Education Magazine*, vol. 12, no. 4, July/August 1995. Reprinted with permission.

Stuart helps his mother assemble his daily medications. He's set the timer on a special watch to remind himself when another dose is due. Additionally, he's researched lymphoma and the popular chemotherapy used in treating various types. He has studied nutrition and holistic methodology. He seems much older than his thirteen years might suggest.

Candi is the homeschooling mother of four. Her youngest children, Maya and Maeve (twins), now three, were born three months early. Being premature, they've required a lot of special care, and are still behind in their development. Maeve has neurological problems and Maya is legally blind. Candi's older children, Ty and Salem, have had to adapt to the extra work the twins have created for the entire family.

At nine, Ty helps with his own curricular preparation. He lists topics he'd like to study, and scours book lists and catalogs for materials. Salem isn't as cooperative. She's a little jealous of her sisters and all of the attention they get.

In an effort to give her "middle child" more devotion, Candi rejected the self-study program that has worked for Ty, knowing Salem's needs are unique to her. Instead, Candi practices "unschooling" principles with her, and encourages Salem to act as a "teacher" for the younger girls.

A Workable Alternative

Each of these families struggle with something unfamiliar to most homeschoolers—the chronically ill or disabled child. How do they do it? In the cases of Karen and Mary, there are few other options. Even in a private school, Tanya would be required to attend for a minimum number of days. And Stuart is often too weak and too sick to accomplish traditional school work.

Candi began homeschooling before the twins were born. For her family, homeschooling is a way of life.

"I can't imagine sending Ty and Salem off on a bus for the entire day," she says. "The twins would be lost without them. In fact, the girls have fared much better than doctors predicted, and I think it's because they have their brother and sister with them all of the time."

> *"Homeschooling is an ideal situation for the family grappling with difficult issues and medical problems."*

Homeschooling is an ideal situation for the family grappling with difficult issues and medical problems. Contrary to what most of us assume, it's no more difficult to "teach" an ill child if flexibility rules the home.

"There are days when Tanya simply is too tired to practice writing or play with the math manipulatives," Karen says, "but on those days we cuddle up with some good books, or pop in a video of a favorite story. We pretty much do year round school at our house."

Mary says, "I don't pressure Stuart. He lets me know what he does or doesn't feel up to. If he wants to help plan dinner, for example, I let him. But, many days he's too nauseous to even think about food. He might hole up in his room and listen to classical music or play computer games."

I wondered if any of the mothers worried that their children weren't learning enough.

"Are you kidding?" Mary laughed, "Stuart knows more about prescription medications than I do!"

Karen agreed, "Tanya seems to be a little more tuned in to learning than the average child her age. For her, it's a fun diversion from feeling tired or ill."

"I really don't have time to worry about what the older two are learning . . . or even if they're learning at all," Candi said. "The twins require so much of me, that we just have a routine and try to be flexible. If Salem is getting out of control, I give her something to do. Something fun. And Ty pretty much just does whatever."

While one might raise an eyebrow to that response, Ty and Salem are bright and articulate children. Ty is

> *"Homeschooling is not only a viable option for these families—it's a strength."*

especially sensitive and considerate, and Salem is very creative. More striking is the gentleness and patience they exhibit towards the twins. For all of her overt jealousy, Salem is a "mother hen" to her younger siblings, keeping Maya out of harm's way and helping Maeve with educational toddler toys.

Clearly, homeschooling is not only a viable option for these families—it's a strength. You and I might have the tendency to feel sorry for these parents, but each one stated that their medical crisis has tightened bonds in their families that homeschooling alone wouldn't have.

"We homeschooled before the twins," Candi repeated, "but it's different now. I'm not 'mom, the teacher'. I'm just 'mom'."

"Don't get me wrong," Mary said, "I hate that my son is so ill. But we've grown so close through all of this. He was in school before, and seemed to be drifting away. He was either at school, with his friends or in front of the TV. Now we do everything together. I just wish it could have happened with him being healthy."

Finding Support

The fear of every parent is illness or harm coming to their child. But if your child is ill or has a disability you can still hold to your convictions regarding homeschooling. In fact, your family can benefit from keeping your child close to hearth and home.

Talk to your child's doctor about education. In Karen's case, Tanya had been missing a lot of school. Her doctor might have suggested tutoring (a common suggestion, by the way) to supplement Tanya's public school education. This is not only expensive, but adequate tutors are difficult to come by.

If your child is seriously ill, most doctors recommend a break from education. The theory is that the child's complete energy can be focused on recovery. Yet, total focus on such a somber topic can prove to have negative effects. The child can become depressed and lethargic, and recovery can actually be impeded. Distraction, in small, measured doses, is often more beneficial for the child (and the parent!).

Support is available for the homeschooling parent of a seriously ill child. America Online has a forum called, "Differently Abled Homeschoolers". If you have a computer and modem, I recommend paying for America Online service for this feature alone. . . .

Think about starting a local Homeschooling Support Group for parents with ill or disabled children. Advertise at your nearby library, YMCA or community center. Post a notice in your church bulletin, asking members to tell others about the program. If you have a small, neighborhood newspaper, place an ad in the classifieds. Ask your doctor to pass the information on to other patients and parents.

Finally, give yourself a break. You have enough to deal with. You don't need to add guilt or pressure to your plate. Don't hold yourself or your child to a rigid school schedule. Don't fret that she's not learning enough. She is. And more importantly, she's learning that you're there—always available whenever she needs you.

Deaf Children Should Not Be Mainstreamed

by Andrew Solomon

About the author: *Andrew Solomon is a contributing writer to the* New York Times Magazine.

The protests at the Lexington Center, which includes New York's oldest Deaf school, are an important stage in the Deaf struggle for civil rights, and on April 25, 1994, the first day of student demonstrations, I ask an African-American from the 11th grade whether she has also demonstrated for race rights. "I'm too busy being Deaf right now," she signs. "My two older brothers aren't Deaf, so they're taking care of being black. Maybe if I have time I'll get to that later."

Deaf and Proud

A Deaf woman standing nearby throws in a question for my benefit: "If you could change being Deaf or being black, which would you do?" The student looks confused, and is suddenly shy. Her signing gets smaller, as though she doesn't want everyone to see it. "Both are hard," she signs back.

Another student intercedes. "I am black and Deaf and proud and I don't want to be white or hearing or different in any way from who I am." Her signs are pretty big and clear. The first student repeats the sign "proud"—her thumb, pointing in, rises up her chest—and then suddenly they are overcome with giggles and go back to join the picket line.

This principle is still new to me, but it has been brewing in the Deaf community for some time: while some deaf people feel cut off from the hearing world, or disabled, for others, being Deaf is a culture and a source of pride. ("Deaf" denotes culture, as distinct from "deaf," which is used to describe a pathology.) A steadily increasing number of deaf people have said that they would not choose to be hearing. To them, the word "cure"—indeed the whole notion of deafness as pathology—is anathema.

My guide here is Jackie Roth, one of the protest's organizers—a Lexington alumna, an actress and an advocate with a practice in cross-cultural sensitivity training for hearing people. Charismatic, self-assured and sharp, she has excellent oral skills and lip-reads well. She speaks and signs simultaneously, which has made her a natural for communicating with the hearing world, and, therefore, an object of suspicion among the Deaf (a position made more difficult by the fact that she has, like many influential Deaf leaders, a hearing spouse). She is unyieldingly ambitious.

"I'm Deaf of Deaf," she says. "I've always said that I'd get to the top and open as many doors as I could for the whole Deaf community. Every deaf child should know he can do anything except hear." Since 90 percent of deaf children are born to hearing parents, Deaf of Deaf carries a certain exclusivity and prestige: Deaf of Deaf have usually grown up understanding from an early age the issues that other deaf people may not take on until much

> *"Every deaf child should know he can do anything except hear."*

later in life. "My father was a dreamer. If he hadn't been deaf, he would have done big things. His family was so ashamed of his being deaf. My mom was a pragmatist, but my father used to say I could do anything. If I said I wanted to be a singer, he never said, 'Deaf girls can't.' He just told me to sing.". . .

Student Protests

An hour after I meet the two proud students, I attend a meeting between the nine-member core committee that organized this protest and the chief executive of the school. Jackie opens. "We do not accept the process by which a new C.E.O. has been named this week to the Lexington Center for the Deaf," she says. "We would like him to resign, and for a new search process to take place." Every detail of the baroquely complex search process is called into question. They want to oust the new chief executive, R. Max Gould, who would oversee the component institutions of the Lexington Center. Most would like to replace him with a Deaf candidate, but whether the new chief executive is Deaf or not, they want him to be approved by the Deaf community.

The center's director of public affairs says that the protests will peter out soon, that students just want an excuse to miss classes, but that is not my impression. "There are no Deaf role models at Lexington," Jackie tells members of the press four days later as the marches continue. Her signs, like her voice, are impatient, quick, funny and fluid. "Few Deaf teachers and even fewer Deaf administrators." The protesters—mostly Lexington students—watch closely. Some are wearing big placards: "The Board Can Hear but They Are Deaf to Us" and "Board Who Can Hear Don't Listen. Those Who Can't Hear Do Listen." Some are wearing "Deaf Pride" T-shirts or buttons. Individuals climb a low wall so everyone can see their rallying cheers, and the crowd chants back to them, many hands moving in repeating patterns.

The faculty representatives to the core committee—Maureen Woods, Jeff Bravin and Janie Moran—are especially vigilant. "Do you think the protest will work?" I ask. Maureen's signing is methodical and impressive. "There is no choice," she says. "It must work." Jeff interrupts. "The pressure has been building, maybe since the school was founded in 1864. Now it's exploding, and nothing can stop it."

A few days later, at another protest, Jeff and his grandmother chat congenially. "My father and my grandfather went to Lexington," Jeff says. "I am Deaf of Deaf of Deaf. We're ready to take what should be ours." Jeff is 25, a member of the "rubella bulge." In the early 60's, a rubella epidemic resulted in a very high incidence of deaf children, and they have made up most of the leadership of the Deaf Pride movement.

Concurrent with these protests, Jackie is giving a performance in the New York Deaf Theater's adaptation of "The Swan." The play describes how a deaf woman of great passion (Jackie) leaves her hearing lover and finds true love with the Swan, who enables her imagination. The lover uses signed English as he speaks; the Swan begins with no language but learns perfect American Sign Language (A.S.L.), the language of the American Deaf, which has its own syntax. Signed English, the use of word signs in English-language word order, is not actually a language at all; cumbersome and slower-paced, it is often used when hearing and deaf people interact. For Jackie's character, love is a liberation from the limitations of hearing culture. As her language, which had suffered the cramp and limitation of her lover's English-oriented signing, opens up into the bodily richness of the Swan's pure A.S.L., she discovers her Deaf self and becomes free.

"I didn't learn real A.S.L. until college," says Jackie, "and what a spreading of the wings it was when it happened! Lexington's tradition of arrogant oralism—they've got a lot to make up for." That Jackie should take so strong a stand against oralism—a philosophy that the deaf should learn to speak like hearing people—is striking, since she is an oral "success story," a woman who can carry on a spoken conversation with little apparent difficulty, who could, if she wanted to, pretty much pass for hearing and who is sometimes dismissed by Deaf purists as "not really Deaf." When Lexington was founded as the first great bastion of oralism in America, it was the idealist wish of hearing people to teach the deaf to speak and read lips so they could function in the "real world" from which they had been excluded. How that dream went horribly wrong is the grand tragedy against which modern Deaf culture has constructed itself.

> *"Signed English, the use of word signs in English-language word order, is not actually a language at all."*

Forbidding Sign

The story of the Deaf is the history of Deaf education, and is recounted in Harlan Lane's *When the Mind Hears*, then analyzed in his *Mask of Benevolence*. These are the seminal texts of the Deaf movement. In 16th-century Spain, for example, only those who had given confession were allowed to inherit property or title, so inbred noble families undertook the oral education of their deaf children. But it was more than 200 years before the Abbé de l'Épée pursued a vocation among the poor deaf of Paris, learned their manual language and used it to teach written French, so freeing the deaf from their prison of illiteracy and isolation.

In 1815, the Rev. Thomas Gallaudet of Connecticut traveled to the institute founded by de l'Épée in Paris, and persuaded Laurent Clerc, a teacher, to accompany him to America to establish a school in Hartford in 1817. A golden age for the American deaf followed. Clerc's French sign language mixed with indigenous American signs and a dialect used on Martha's Vineyard (where there was much hereditary deafness) to form American Sign Language. Deaf people wrote books, entered public life, achieved. Gallaudet College was founded to provide the highest advanced education to the deaf and is still the world's only Deaf university.

> *"The insistence on teaching English only . . . served not to raise deaf literacy, but to lower it."*

In *Seeing Voices,* Oliver Sacks suggests that once the deaf were seen to function so broadly, it was natural that they should be asked to speak. Alexander Graham Bell led the oralist movement, which culminated with the dread Congress of Milan in 1880 and an edict to ban the use of sign. The insistence on teaching English only (which prevailed until the 1980's; "I got my hands rapped if I signed," Jackie recalls) served not to raise deaf literacy, but to lower it.

Forbidding sign turned children not toward spoken English, but away from language. "We felt retarded," Jackie says. "Everything depended on one completely boring skill, and we were all bad at it. Some bright kids who didn't have that talent just became dropouts." Even those who developed pronunciation lost out. "History lessons," Jackie says. "We spent two weeks learning to say 'guillotine' and that was what we learned about the French Revolution. Then you go out and say 'guillotine' to someone with your deaf voice, and they haven't the slightest idea what you're talking about—usually they can't tell what you're trying to pronounce when you say 'Coke' at McDonald's."

Learning was supposed to happen through lip reading, a remarkably inexact science; most lip movements are associated with more than one sound, and the lip reader must guess and intuit in order to make sense of what is being said. "Pat, mat, bat," Jackie mouthed. "Now, did I say the same word three times or did I say three different words?" For someone who already speaks English— someone deafened postlingually—the technique can be developed, but for someone with limited English, it is an excruciating endeavor. "Socially or in secret," Jackie says, "we always signed. No theory could kill our language."

Though at least 30 percent of deafness is genetic, more than 90 percent of deaf children are born to hearing parents. So most deaf children enter families that neither understand nor know their situation. They must identify in their peer group; they are first exposed to Deaf ways in school. When you meet a deaf person, his school is a primary mode of self-identification; it's usually told after his name but before his job. "Lexington" and "Gallaudet" were among the first signs I learned.

A Distinct Language

The Deaf debates are all language debates. "When I communicate in A.S.L., my native language," M.J. Bienvenu, a political activist, said to me, "I am living my culture. I don't define myself in terms of 'not hearing' or of 'not' anything else." A founder of the Bicultural Center (a sort of Deaf think tank), M.J. is gracious, but also famously terrifying: brilliant, striking-looking and self-possessed, with signing so swift, crisp and perfectly controlled that she seems to be rearranging the air in front of her into a more acceptable shape. Deaf of Deaf, with Deaf sisters, she manifests, like many other activists, a pleasure in American Sign Language that only poets feel for English. "When our language was acknowledged," she says, "we gained our freedom." In her hands "freedom"—clenched hands are crossed before the body, then swing apart and face out—is like an explosion.

The fact that A.S.L. is a full (though not written) language, with a logical internal grammar and the capacity to express anything that can be expressed verbally, eluded scholars until William Stokoe published his ground-breaking *Sign Language Structure* in 1960. This became the basis for the Deaf activism of which Lexington's is the most recent example. "To establish the validity of A.S.L.," Stokoe says, "we had to spend a long time dwelling on how it resembles spoken language. Now that the validity of A.S.L. has been accepted, we can concentrate on what's interesting—how the life perceptions and experiences of a native A.S.L.-user will differ from the perceptions and experiences of hearing people." Or, as M.J. put it, "There are many things that I can experience for which you have no equivalent."

> *"Forbidding sign turned children not toward spoken English, but away from language."*

Perception of A.S.L. uses the language center of the brain more than the visual-emotion center. Deaf children show no predisposition to spoken language; they respond intuitively to sign, and acquire it exactly as hearing children acquire spoken languages. During the critical period for language acquisition—at its height between 18 and 36 months, dwindling around 12 years—the mind can internalize the principles of grammar and signification. This paves the way for human thought. (There is no rich abstraction without words.)

Once you have learned one language, you can go on, at any age, to learn more or other languages. Spoken-written language can readily be taught to the deaf as a second language. But to bring up deaf children without sign models is terribly dangerous. Though some remarkable ones acquire English through lip reading and residual hearing with constant attention, more often deaf children without exposure to sign bypass the key age for language acquisition without really acquiring any language at all. Once that happens, they frequently fail to develop full cognitive skills; they may suffer permanently from what has been described as a preventable form of mental retardation.

> *"Deaf children show no predisposition to spoken language; they respond intuitively to sign."*

Helen Keller famously observed that being blind cuts people off from things, while being deaf cuts people off from other people. Poor communication skills result in psychosis; the National Institutes of Health had a workshop in June 1994 on the link between poor hearing (nonsigners) and violence. Deaf of Deaf learn sign as a first language at home and are often surprised to discover that other systems of communication are used elsewhere. For the deaf children of hearing parents, school is often the place where they first encounter sign. It is not just social or intellectual stimulation that school may provide; when it is the beginning of language, school is the first awakening of the mind. As I slide deeper into Deaf culture by way of the Lexington protests, I see how a language has defined a system of thought—and I begin to imagine what M.J. may be able to experience that I may not.

A Civil Rights Movement

On Monday May 2, 1994, the demonstrators go to the Queens Borough President's office. It is a beautiful, sunny day, and the demonstration, though still in deadly earnest, has that air of festivity that clings to anything for which people are skipping work or school. Jackie Roth is holding forth, and so are a variety of distinguished Deaf leaders. And Greg Hlibok, a leader of the Deaf President Now movement, is expected.

In March 1988, Gallaudet University, the center of American Deaf culture, announced the appointment of a new president. Students had rallied for the school to have its first Deaf president, but the chairman, remarking that "the deaf are not yet ready to function in the hearing world," announced that a hearing candidate had been selected.

In the following week, the Deaf community as a political force came abruptly into its own. The movement that had begun with Stokoe's validation of A.S.L. took its next great leap forward. The Deaf President Now movement made it clear that the Deaf community was able to function at any level it chose. In a week, they closed down the university, won substantial coverage in the media and staged a march on the Capitol with 2,500 supporters. The chairman resigned, and her place was taken by Jeff Bravin's father, Phil Bravin (who is also on the Lexington board). The board immediately named the first Deaf president of Gallaudet, I. King Jordan. Late-deafened in a motorcycle accident at 21, King Jordan is the most unaffectedly bicultural person I have met; against all the predictions of the hearing world, he has proved a remarkable leader while vastly increasing the school's endowment.

Deaf President Now is Lexington's inspiration. At the Borough President's office, Hlibok is electrifying. An articulate signer can build up a picture in front of himself, and the iconic content of A.S.L. provides much of its immediacy and power. Like M.J., Hlibok takes over a substantial block of space in front of himself when he signs. He says that the Lexington board members are like adults playing with a doll house, moving deaf students like dolls. He seems to create the house in the air; by the time he has finished, you can see it and the interfering arms of the board reaching into it. It is as if his fingers have left trails of light behind them that hold the pictures he is drawing. His wrists snap sharply with conviction, and his hands open and close as if they might eventually stop in the shape of fists. The students cheer, many of them by raising their hands over their heads and waving them, fingers splayed, in Deaf applause.

Victory

In the midst of the Lexington fracas, Max Gould, the newly appointed chief executive, resigns. There are waves of astonishment. Gould claims that his appointment has been muddying the real issues facing Lexington. Seizing the air of opportunity, a board member proposes Phil Bravin as board president, and the incumbent withdraws. The Gallaudet scenario has repeated itself. Many Deaf people, when they are very excited, make loud sounds, often at very high or very low pitches, wordless exclamations of delight. In the halls of Lexington, students cheer, almost incredulous that their actions could have been fruitful, and anyone hearing is transfixed by the sound.

"It was a real sense of déjà vu," Phil Bravin would say to me one afternoon a few months later. "It was so much like Gallaudet all over again, and it showed that that victory was just the beginning. It was also the best thing that could have happened to those students, no matter how many classes they missed during the protests. You can't learn civil rights from a textbook. Some of them came from families that said, 'You're deaf; don't shoot too high.' Now they know better."

"To bring up deaf children without sign models is terribly dangerous."

At Lexington graduation, a week later, Hlibok is the speaker. In the midst of a hackneyed, boring speech, he says, rather casually, "From the time God made earth until today, this is probably the best time to be Deaf." At a victory celebration the next day, Jeff Bravin says, "We'll be running our own show now." Jackie Roth says: "It's all great. But the battle's not over." And indeed, within a month a new saga will begin over the appointment of a principal for J.H.S. 47, New York City's only public school for the deaf; once more, the Deaf will be excluded from the selection process.

A Rejection of Mainstreaming

"Mainstreaming" (or "inclusion")—"the backlash," as M.J. Bienvenu calls it—is making schools ever more the locus of Deaf struggles. The Americans With Disabilities Act, in an attempt to give full educational benefits to people once shunted into second-rate special schools, has recommended that schools be made more fully accessible. Public law 94-142 maintains that everyone who can use ordinary schools should do so. For the deaf, often physically unable to learn the mainstream's means of communication, this is the worst disaster since the Congress of Milan. "Children from Spanish-speaking homes may learn English at school as a second language," says M.J. "Children from nonsigning homes who are taught only in English at school may never learn language at all." The Clinton Administration has not been receptive to calls for separate Deaf schools. "It is a terrible abuse," says Oscar Cohen, Lexington's superintendent. Jackie Roth says, "It makes me sick with rage."

"There are some children who can function well in mainstream schools," says Robert Davila, an Assistant Secretary of Education under George Bush and a leader of the Hispanic Deaf community. "They need help from supportive families, special abilities, good language of some kind and constant individual help from teachers. Many children, even if they overcome the incredible obstacles, will be so lonely there. The Deaf school where I went was my salvation."

According to the Rowley decision, which upheld a school district's refusal to provide interpreter services to a deaf girl on grounds that she was passing, it is the obligation of the schools into which children are mainstreamed to give "sufficient" education rather than to "maximize" those students' potential. Their social welfare is not a concern.

> *"For the deaf, often physically unable to learn the mainstream's means of communication, [inclusion] is [a] disaster."*

Once considered the vanguard of Deaf separatism, M.J. Bienvenu's Bicultural Center now focuses on cooperation; it laid the groundwork for the Bi-Bi (bilingual, bicultural) movement in education, which is the Deaf community's answer to mainstreaming and an alternative to the trend in Deaf education for "total communication."

"Total communication" means speaking and signing at once, and it's difficult to do. Non-A.S.L. signed languages, predicated on oral syntax as they are, are sometimes nearly incomprehensible. And the structures of English and A.S.L. are completely different; you can no more speak English while signing in A.S.L. than you can speak English while writing Chinese. In English, words are used in sequence; A.S.L. often uses words simultaneously, or amalgamates them into composite signs. So in A.S.L., one gesture could mean "He moved from the East Coast to the West Coast." If you sign "he," then "moved," then "from" and so on, logic disappears; a visual grammar conveyed sequentially is "unnatural" and counterintuitive.

In Bi-Bi, children are encouraged to develop sign as a "natural" first language; written English is taught as a second language, and many students seem to excel at it, running close to their hearing counterparts. (It should be noted that, on average, deaf high-school graduates have a fourth-grade reading level.) The technique is gaining: Eddy Laird, superintendent of the Indiana School for the Deaf, has been one of the first to institute Bi-Bi on a full scale. It has also been used at the schools on the Gallaudet campus.

> *"Those who learn forced English while being denied sign emerge semilingual."*

Spoken English is taught but not emphasized within the Bi-Bi system. The system's successes are astonishing, and yet the lack of spoken language is a real disability. It is striking that many of the most extreme anti-oralists themselves have and use excellent oral skills. "They're incredibly useful, and anyone who can learn them should," Jackie Roth acknowledged. "I happen to have a skill there, and it's been invaluable for me. But speech can't be taught at the cost of human growth. Balance!". . .

Issues About Language and Ability

I attend the 1994 biennial National Association of the Deaf convention, which takes place this year in Knoxville, Tenn., with almost 2,000 Deaf participants. At Lexington, I saw Deaf people stand up to the hearing world. I learned how a TTY (a telephone cum typewriter device for the Deaf) works, met pet dogs who understood sign, talked about mainstreaming and oralism and the integrity of visual language. I became accustomed to doorbells that flashed lights instead of ringing. But none of this could have prepared me for the immersion that is the N.A.D. convention, where the brightest, most politicized, most committed Deaf gather for political focus and social exchange. The association has been the center of Deaf self-realization and power since it was founded in 1880. . . .

Gary Mowl, head of the A.S.L. department at National Technical Institute of the Deaf, has come to the conference with his children. He often corrects their grammar and usage in A.S.L. The importance of having a correct language— "Gallaudet A.S.L.," an answer to standard English—has only recently been recognized. "People ask why you need to teach A.S.L. to native signers. Why do English-speaking students study English?" I think of the sign used by the Deaf gangs of Harlem and the East Village, which is completely incomprehensible to an A.S.L.-user. . . .

I get into a lot of conversations about interpreters: the shortage of competent interpreters is appalling. There is always competition between CODA (Children of Deaf Adults; refers only to hearing people) professional interpreters and non-CODA ones. The complexities and ambivalences of CODA-Deaf relations, humorously but knowingly conveyed by Lou Ann Walker in *A Loss for Words,* are a big part of Deaf culture. (I have the good fortune to work with a CODA named Marie Taccogna, a gifted interpreter who translates both language and culture.) At public meetings, there are often interpreters who are "doing some kind of a dance," says Rob Roth, who is at the National Association of the Deaf to represent AT&T, "which is lovely as interpretive performance but conveys no information in a language I speak. Hearing people love their picturesque eloquence.". . .

Who's Disabled?

I am talking to Alec Naiman, whom I first met at Lexington. A world traveler, he was one of the pilots in 1994's Deaf fly-in at the Knoxville airport. We discuss a trip he made to China. "I met some Deaf Chinese people my first day, and went to stay with them. Deaf people never need hotels; you can always stay with other Deaf people. We spoke different signed languages, but we could make ourselves understood. Though we came from different countries, Deaf culture held us together. By the end of the evening we'd talked about Deaf life in China, and about Chinese politics, and we'd understood each other linguistically and culturally." I nod. "No hearing American could do that in China," he says. "So who's disabled then?". . .

How to reconcile this Deaf experience with the rest of the world? Should it be reconciled at all? M.J. Bienvenu has been one of the most vocal and articulate opponents of the language of disability. "I am Deaf," she says to me in Knoxville, drawing out the sign for "Deaf," the index finger moving from chin to ear, as though she is tracing a broad smile. "To see myself as Deaf is as much of a choice as it is for me to be a lesbian. I have identified with my culture, taken a public stand, made myself a figure within this community." Considerably gentler now than in her extremist heyday in the early 80's, she acknowledges that "for some deaf people, being deaf is a disability. Those who learn forced English while being denied sign emerge semilingual rather than bilingual, and they are disabled people. But for the rest of us, it is no more a disability than being Japanese would be."

Chapter 4

What Medical Responses to Disability Are Acceptable?

Chapter Preface

On January 23, 1996, at the Stanford University Medical Center in Palo Alto, California, 34-year-old Sandra Jensen underwent a heart and lung transplant—an operation she had fought long and hard to obtain. Jensen has Down's syndrome, a chromosomal disorder that usually results in mental retardation and often causes congenital heart defects. Today, most children with the Down's syndrome heart defect undergo corrective surgery, but when Jensen was born this medical technique was unavailable. Over the years, her heart and lungs deteriorated to the point that she could not survive without an organ transplant, and she applied to the waiting lists of the transplant programs at Stanford and at the University of California at San Diego (UCSD) Medical Center.

However, because of the long waiting lists for heart-lung transplants, hospitals regularly reject patients who are not considered to be good candidates for survival. Both Stanford and UCSD turned down Jensen's application, citing her mental disability and questioning whether she could follow the stringent postoperative regime of medication, self-monitoring, and exercises. Stanford's rejection letter stated, "We do not feel that patients with Down's syndrome are appropriate candidates for heart-lung transplantion."

Jensen, her family, and a group of supporters claimed that the hospitals were discriminating on the basis of disability. For several years, they pointed out, Jensen had successfully lived on her own, held down a part-time job, and worked as an advocate for the rights of the disabled. Philip Bach, her family doctor, maintained that Jensen already followed a pill-taking schedule and was more than capable of monitoring her health. The hospitals' decisions, Jensen's advocates argued, were founded on biased views of people with Down's syndrome and did not take Jensen's individual capabilities into account. Frank Murphy, director of the National Down Syndrome Congress, asserted that the hospitals were "making a value-of-life judgment that they don't have any right to make." Both hospitals countered that there was nothing discriminatory or unethical about their decisions. According to Bruce A. Reitz, the head of Stanford's transplant program, "everyone has to meet certain norms" for a place on the waiting list. Nevertheless, Stanford reconsidered Jensen's case and Reitz performed the successful operation.

Jensen's story illustrates the difficulty in determining what medical responses to disability are appropriate, especially in life-or-death situations. Medical personnel, people with disabilities, and other concerned individuals grapple with ethical questions about such issues as the abortion of disabled fetuses, genetic testing for disabilities, assisted suicide, and euthanasia. The authors of the following viewpoints debate which medical responses to disability are most humane.

Genetic Testing Can Reduce Disabilities

by Joseph Levine and David Suzuki

About the authors: *Joseph Levine is a biologist at Boston College and a journalist specializing in scientific topics. David Suzuki is a geneticist at the University of British Columbia and the author of several books.*

When Tessie Ashe was eighteen years old, she watched her nine-year-old niece, Farrell, die of cystic fibrosis (CF). In the grip of that fatal genetic disorder, Farrell spent much of her brief life fighting for every breath she drew. Her physical problem was as simple as it was implacable: she was being strangled by her own lungs. The cells lining her respiratory tract, their normal function impaired by a defective gene, secreted a thick, viscous mucus that blocked the flow of air. Farrell was so dependent on supplemental oxygen that she gasped and struggled like a fish out of water during the few seconds it took her mother to switch her mask to a new supply tank. By the time she succumbed to the disease, she weighed barely forty-nine pounds.

A Deadly Disease

As traumatic as Farrell's death was, her suffering upset her aunt Tessie Ashe even more. Being forced to watch helplessly while the child lived in constant pain was almost more than Ashe could bear. So years later, when their son, Paul, was born, Tessie and Kevin Ashe banished from their minds the possibility that he could have the disease. Their optimism seemed reasonable; their first child, Emily, was a perfectly healthy two-year-old.

But Paul failed to gain weight normally despite constant feeding and had serious digestive problems and salty-tasting skin, all hallmarks of cystic fibrosis. Within weeks, the anxious parents found themselves in the all too familiar environs of the hospital where Farrell had died. When they received the awful news that Paul, too, had CF, Tessie Ashe felt as though she had been punched in the stomach. "You've just given my baby a death sentence!" she cried at the pediatrician. Sadly, the Ashes have a great deal of company in their distress; cystic fibrosis is one of the most common inherited diseases, striking one in every twenty-five hundred Caucasian newborns in the United States.

Symptoms of CF, like those of sickle-cell anemia, appear only in individuals burdened with two copies of a mutant gene. People like Tessie and Kevin Ashe, who carry one normal and one defective copy, may

> *"Several lines of [genetic] research . . . hold the promise of effective treatment and possibly even a cure for [cystic fibrosis]."*

never learn of the danger that lurks in their DNA unless they marry one another and have children. In those situations, half the mother's eggs and half the father's sperm carry the deadly allele. The probability that an unlucky egg will meet a similarly unlucky sperm is 25 percent, so each child conceived by CF carriers has a one in four chance of getting cystic fibrosis.

Thus Paul's diagnosis was a diagnosis for the entire Ashe family; it meant that both Tessie and Kevin were CF carriers and that any future child of theirs would face those odds in a potentially lethal round of genetic Russian roulette. That made the blow even harder to take, for the Ashes had dreamed of a large family. But under the circumstances, they would never try to conceive again. "The natural course is for my children to bury me," says Kevin Ashe. "I'd like to keep it that way."

Then, two weeks after the Ashes received the grim news about Paul, a scientific breakthrough lifted the pall of gloom that had settled over their future. In what the Ashes see as the work of God, researchers located and identified the gene that causes cystic fibrosis. Suddenly their family was thrust into the high-technology world of molecular genetics—a world in which constant advances raise both hopes about medical miracles and fears of social abuses. Some of those advances are already enabling the Ashes to fulfill their dream of a large, healthy family. Moreover, several lines of research, though still in experimental stages, hold the promise of effective treatment and possibly even a cure for CF during Paul's lifetime. . . .

Testing for Genetic Disorders

The most clear-cut medical technique for avoiding the birth of children with genetic diseases—and the only one available until recently—is both physically and psychologically traumatic. The procedure involves collecting fetal cells from the womb by amniocentesis eighteen weeks into pregnancy, and performing a genetic test for the mutant gene on those cells. Should the test reveal that the embryo carries the deadly mutation, abortion is considered. That course of action, however, was never open to the Ashes, whose religious beliefs include unshakable adherence to an anti-abortion philosophy. "We would not abort," Tessie Ashe asserts emphatically. "That's not an option for us."

But new, extraordinarily sensitive genetic testing methods, facilitated by the discovery of the CF gene, offer Tessie and Kevin the hope of bearing children free of cystic fibrosis through a procedure with which they can personally feel more comfortable. The technique, *preimplantation diagnosis*, is still experimental and not predictable enough to guarantee success. But the Ashes have traveled to London to join the handful of willing experimental subjects at Hammersmith Hospital. "To have a healthy child," Tessie affirms, "I would go to the ends of the earth."

The key to the Hammersmith procedure is the hospital's highly respected *in vitro fertilization* (IVF) clinic, originally set up to serve infertile couples. Normally, the female member undergoes several weeks of hormone treatments, which induce her ovaries to release numerous eggs. Those eggs are harvested, then joined with the husband's sperm in a glass dish. Viable embryos selected from the resulting fertilized eggs are then implanted into the mother's uterus.

The Ashes are hardly infertile—"I think about becoming pregnant and I become pregnant," laughs Tessie. But they, too, will undergo in vitro fertilization, with the addition of one critical step. Their fertilized eggs, rather than being implanted at random, will be incubated for three days, coddled in culture as they grow into clusters of eight cells. Those eight-cell embryos then become the subjects of what is arguably the most delicate operation ever performed on human tissues. First, microscopic instruments are used to bore a tiny hole in the protective layer surrounding the embryo. Then an equally microscopic syringe removes a single cell, which is rushed to the laboratory for genetic testing. Using the polymerase chain reaction (PCR) technique, lab personnel make millions of copies of that cell's DNA, providing enough genetic material to facilitate a search for the CF mutation in the embryo's genome. Only embryos determined to be free of CF will be implanted into Tessie's uterus. There, with luck, at least one will develop into a normal baby. . . .

> *"Extraordinarily sensitive genetic testing methods . . . offer [cystic fibrosis carriers] the hope of bearing children free of cystic fibrosis."*

Not the Same as Abortion

By 1992, when Tessie and Kevin Ashe arrived at the clinic, six perfectly normal babies had been born after undergoing preimplantation diagnosis for other genetic diseases. Buoyed by that information, and after a great deal of thought and heartfelt prayer, the Ashes decided that preimplantation diagnosis was not only their best option, but that it was also consistent with their religious convictions.

For one thing, the Ashes have been assured that up to 80 percent of human embryos at the eight-cell stage don't implant successfully in the uterine wall, even under completely natural conditions. Those embryos are normally sloughed off by the body without their would-be mother even knowing that any of her eggs had been fertilized. In a sense, therefore, the selection process of preimplantation diagnosis occurs at, or before, the stage of development during which a similar, though more random, weeding-out process occurs in nature.

Furthermore, because each of the eight cells in this early embryonic cluster is totally undifferentiated, the Ashes can think about them very differently than they would about the parts of an embryo further along in development. "I feel comfortable with this," Tessie explains, "because each cell does not know where it is going to be. It's not as if there is a beating heart or a brain wave, so at this point I feel more comfortable with it than I would terminating a pregnancy."

Numerous other members of the large and diverse prolife movement, however, disagree with this rational assessment. Such individuals believe that human life is sacred from the moment of conception onward and insist that no interference with the reproductive process is permissible. What such people would say to parents of children suffering with CF is unclear. Whether they would change their views if forced to live with such suffering on a daily basis, and to weigh the affliction of genetic disease against the joy of parenthood, is also an open question. Science per se has little to contribute to such intensely personal judgments.

Giving Hope to Families

Though preimplantation diagnosis is controversial in some circles, to many observers it is both a major biomedical advance and one of the more benign procedures to emerge from the reading of human genes. Its application so far is restricted to a small, well-defined population: couples who know that they are carriers of an inherited disease whose genetic basis has been identified. The procedure's goal is humanitarian and economically sensible: enabling such couples to conceive children while avoiding the trauma and financial burden of lethal hereditary ailments.

Genetic Testing for Disabilities Is Unethical

by Marta Russell

About the author: *Marta Russell is a freelance writer and a media consultant on disability issues.*

Rarely have I felt my life to be so devalued as when I attended a workshop in Irvine, California, with experts in genetic diagnosis, testing and screening services. I have had cerebral palsy from birth, so I am not a rookie or wilting flower when it comes to oppressive attitudes toward people with disabilities. So why did I feel so overwhelmed at this conference? Because this struck at my core—my own right to exist in this world.

Who Should Judge?

Genetic prenatal screening, originally restricted by the medical profession to the detection of severe "defects," has become a search-and-destroy mission for those who can afford it, offering the chance for parents to abort any "abnormal" fetus or even a fetus of an unwanted sex. Even those states that restrict such abortions allow them in the case of a "severe" or "grave" defect in the fetus. Although I remain pro-choice, there is an affront to my own worth when fetuses are valued for the degree of their physical or mental acceptability. Who judges what a potential life is worth?

Although the workshop presented an array of professionals who talked of the ethics of screening decisions, there was not one disabled person originally on the committee. It was generally agreed that serious chromosome abnormalities such as Down's Syndrome and Tay-Sachs were targets for abortion. Other diseases under discussion were anencephaly, sickle cell anemia and spina bifida. But whatever guidelines the "experts" deem appropriate, individuals will make the final decisions, influenced by subtle societal pressures.

Now that physicians can diagnose a disability in the womb, there is much societal pressure to have a "perfect" baby, which further stigmatizes an infant

Marta Russell, "Genetic Screening: Who Judges What Life Is Worth?" *Los Angeles Times*, February 22, 1993. Reprinted by permission of the author.

who does have a disability. Mothers still bear most of the responsibility for raising children, and there is little in the way of in-home support services for children with disabilities. Women do not want—or can't afford—to sacrifice their careers and return home full-time to care for children with disabilities. In an era where social support systems are being literally wiped out by budget cuts and with health costs still soaring, the costs associated with raising a child with a disability appear larger than life. And it is likely that in the future, insurance companies will consider a genetically diagnosed prenatal disability a "preexistent" condition and refuse to cover the infant at all.

Anti-Disability Sentiments

One day while in my physical therapist's gym, I heard a young woman talking with one of the therapists about her failed attempts at finding a baby to adopt. She was casually complaining to the therapist that the only baby she had been offered was an infant with a club foot. The therapist tried to explain to her that this was a fairly simple matter to handle, but the young woman insisted that she did not feel that she could financially or emotionally cope with that sort of "problem."

Anti-disability sentiment was expressed publicly in 1992 when CBS anchor Bree Walker was openly attacked on KFI radio for electing to have her baby, despite a good chance that it would inherit her disability. The question posed was: Should Bree Walker have conceived a child? Talk show host Jane Norris asked her audience, "Is that a fair thing to do? Is it fair for Bree Walker to deliver this child?" Since Walker has the genetic disability (a fusing of the bones in her hands), hers was an informed choice. The public attack against her for making this choice exposed the deep fear, anxiety and misunderstanding of disability in our culture.

> *"Genetic prenatal screening . . . has become a search-and-destroy mission."*

We need to ask what kind of a society creates parents who feel that having a child with a disability is not an option for them? What kind of a culture views disability as a burden placed on society, stigmatizing children who happen to have a disability?

In the 1940s, Nazi Germany, with the agreement of highly regarded German physicians, built its first gas chambers in mental institutions to eliminate the mentally retarded. German social policy sought to rectify the disorderliness of nature, to relieve the state and the family of the burden of caring for the unproductive. The killing later spread to the physically disabled, schizophrenics, manic-depressives, alcoholics and other socially "undesirable" folks—an eventual total of 250,000 children and adults in this category. How many "defects" will genetic prenatal screening eventually deem fatal?

Genetic Testing and Eugenics

Let us not confuse the prevention of a disease with the elimination of one through the practice of eugenics. These parents choosing abortion rarely think of their actions as partaking in eugenics—a social and economic theory that calls for "perfecting" the human gene pool by eliminating "defective" off-spring—but in effect they are.

My mother had German measles in her first trimester, which was believed to have caused my cerebral palsy. My parents could have chosen to eliminate me had prenatal screening been available in the 1950s. It is ironic that when people with disabilities now have federal laws to protect them against discrimination in the workplace and in our environment (Americans with Disabilities Act), that there will be fewer and fewer of us to make use of the victory many of us have waged our entire lives to win—the right to equality in the eyes of the nation.

Progressive science has brought us many positive benefits. Undoubtedly, human genome research will add to those benefits. But people with disabilities must be alert and active participants in the debate about an oversight of this growing research.

Euthanasia of Disabled Infants Is Morally Acceptable

by Peter Singer

About the author: *Peter Singer teaches philosophy and ethics at Monash University in Melbourne, Australia. The following viewpoint is excerpted from his book* Rethinking Life and Death: The Collapse of Our Traditional Ethics.

Very many severely disabled infants, especially those who are judged to have poor prospects of a life of reasonable quality, and who are unwanted by their parents, are deliberately treated in such a way that they die rapidly and without suffering. Perhaps the clearest illustration of the way in which doctors have found themselves unable to work within the framework of the traditional sanctity of life ethic [the belief that all life is sacred and should be preserved in every case] comes from the treatment of babies born with spina bifida.

Treating Spina Bifida

Spina bifida means, literally, a 'divided spine'. In serious cases, the baby is born with a part of its spine split and the spinal cord exposed. The nerves which run along the spine will then be damaged. The result is partial or complete paralysis of the legs, and no ability to control the bowel or bladder. The spine may also be deformed. Intellectual disability is often present in people seriously affected by spina bifida, but by no means always. Spina bifida is one of the more common birth defects. It used to be said to occur in about one birth in every thousand, but better nutrition, especially folic acid, has been shown to reduce its incidence. In addition, some cases are detected during pregnancy with the result that they do not come to birth.

Until the 1950s, almost all babies born with spina bifida died soon after birth. Sometimes this was because midwives and family doctors made sure that they did not live; but even if the doctors did their best, the open wound over the spine was sure to become infected, and in the days before antibiotics, this was likely to prove fatal. Operating on the baby to close the wound on the spine only meant that the cerebro-spinal fluid which would have leaked out of the wound now built up in the brain, where it caused the baby's head to swell, and often led to brain damage. In the 1950s, however, antibiotics became available, and a way was found to drain the cerebro-spinal fluid into the bloodstream. Suddenly it was possible to save the lives of thousands of children who would otherwise have died.

At this point Dr John Lorber enters the story. Lorber was a paediatrician in Sheffield, an industrial city in the north of England that had a high rate of spina bifida. Lorber was at first enthusiastic about the new mode of treating these babies. In 1963, together with two colleagues, he published an influential paper stating that every infant with spina bifida must be operated on as soon as possible since otherwise further nerve damage could occur. In Sheffield and in many other centres in Britain and America this was the way spina bifida was handled for the next few years. The parents were rarely consulted about this decision— they were simply told that their baby needed an operation, and given a form to sign. But the operation to close the wound at the back of the spine was only the beginning of the treatment. After that a tube with a one-way valve was installed to drain the excess cerebro-spinal fluid from the head into the bloodstream. Then orthopaedic operations were needed to correct deformities of the spine and hip. Some children needed thirty or forty orthopaedic operations before they had finished school.

Doubts About the Quality of Life

After a decade of universal active treatment of all babies with spina bifida, Lorber began to have doubts about what he and his colleagues were doing. He analysed the records of the 848 children they had treated in Sheffield. Half had died, most of these during the first year of life. Of those who had survived, only six had no handicap, and seventy-three were only moderately handicapped. More than 80 per cent were severely handicapped: that is, they had at least two, but usually more, of the following conditions: no bowel and bladder control, or a urinary bypass with frequent kidney infections and progressive chronic kidney damage which sometimes led to kidney failure; paralysis to such a degree that they were unable to walk without caliper splints, crutches, or other appliances and had to rely on a wheelchair for part of the day; pressure sores on feet, knees, or buttocks; hydrocephalus which was treated by a drainage tube, requiring new operations to deal with frequent complications. In addition to these physical problems, approximately one-third of the surviving children were intellectually disabled.

> *"Very many severely disabled infants . . . are deliberately treated in such a way that they die rapidly and without suffering."*

In the light of these figures, Lorber decided that the initial enthusiasm for the new mode of treatment had led to its being used without sufficient reflection. He called for a reassessment of priorities 'to ensure that, with all the intensive effort and good will, we shall not do more harm than good'. He suggested a more selective policy. He went back through the records and found that the size and location of the opening over the spine were, along with other medical indications, good predictors of the severity of the disability that the child would have. He therefore proposed that infants with spina bifida should be examined for 'adverse criteria' that indicated the virtual certainty of severe disability. If the medical team had concentrated its efforts on treating only infants without any of these adverse criteria, all those who survived with nothing worse than a moderate handicap would have received treatment.

> *"Until the 1950s, almost all babies born with spina bifida died soon after birth."*

Endorsing Selective Treatment

That left an obvious question: what should happen to the others—the majority of babies with spina bifida—who would not be actively treated? Lorber's answer was clear. 'No treatment' meant that nothing should be done to prolong their lives. The wound should be left open. If an infection developed, no antibiotics should be given. If excess fluid accumulated in the head, this should not be drained. If the babies did not eat and lost weight, they should not be tube-fed. Instead they should be kept comfortable and free from pain. In these circumstances, Lorber felt able to predict, very few, if any, would live longer than six months.

Lorber presented his case for a selective approach in the *British Medical Journal* in 1971 and 1972. The pendulum of medical opinion then began to swing away from universal intervention. In a leading article, the *Medical Journal of Australia* endorsed selective treatment for spina bifida. Medical teams in Oxford, Edinburgh and Melbourne published details of their own selective treatment practices. In 1973 Drs Raymond Duff and A.G.M. Campbell, writing of the need to break down 'the public and professional silence on a major social taboo', published in the *New England Journal of Medicine* the details of 299 deaths of infants under their care in Yale–New Haven Hospital. Of these, forty-three, including seven cases of spina bifida, were the result of a decision to withhold medical treatments. The British government's department of health and social security endorsed selective treatment. It was also supported at meetings of spina bifida associations, consisting of parents of children with spina bifida, and social workers and others connected with the people with the condition.

Since that period, the selective treatment of spina bifida infants has been normal practice in many paediatric hospitals in most of the developed world. Some doctors continue to be opposed to it, and do not practise it. Others think that Lorber's criteria exclude too many children with good prospects of an acceptable quality of life. Undoubtedly, since Lorber published his proposals, new ways of treating spina bifida have made it easier for some people to cope with the condition. It would be surprising if any medical criteria for treatment or non-treatment remained unchanged for twenty years. The issue with which we are concerned, however, is not the details of the criteria for selection, but the principle of selective non-treatment itself. As long as we think that there are some cases in which it is acceptable, we are accepting a quality of life ethic [the belief that the quality of a patient's life should be considered in determining the course of medical treatment].

Support for Infant Euthanasia

Surveys of paediatricians and obstetricians have consistently shown that the doctors who treat newborn infants support selective non-treatment. In 1975 a questionnaire was sent to all 400 paediatric surgeons in the surgical section of the American Academy of Pediatrics, and 308 chairpersons of teaching departments of paediatrics. The response rate was nearly two-thirds.The first question was: 'Do you believe that the life of each and every newborn infant should be saved if it is within our ability to do so?' Only 18 per cent of those responding answered in the affirmative, the remaining 82 per cent indicating that they did not believe that we should save every newborn infant. Other questions described various situations and asked the doctors what they would do. For instance, in the situation [of] a Down syndrome infant with a blockage of the digestive system, and parents who refused permission for surgery, 77 per cent of the surgeons and 50 per cent of the general paediatricians said that they would not oppose the parents' refusal. Moreover, even among those respondents who said that they would oppose the refusal, most would limit this opposition to attempts to persuade the parents to change their mind. Only 3 per cent of the surgeons and 16 per cent of the paediatricians said that they would go to the lengths of getting a court order to allow the operation to go ahead. In two other American surveys carried out in California and Massachusetts, a majority of paediatricians said that they would not recommend surgery for a Down syndrome infant with a life-threatening blockage in its intestine. These views may not be very different from those of the American public as a whole. In a 1983 Gallup poll, Americans were asked what they would do if they had a badly deformed baby in need of treatment. Forty-three per cent said that they would ask the doctor not to keep the baby alive, and 40 per cent said they would want the baby kept alive. . . .

> *"After a decade of universal active treatment of all babies with spina bifida, [Dr John] Lorber began to have doubts about what he and his colleagues were doing."*

A Traditional, Worldwide Practice

Killing unwanted infants or allowing them to die has been a normal practice in most societies throughout human history and prehistory. We find it, for example, in ancient Greece, where disabled infants were exposed on the mountainside. We find it in nomadic tribes like the Kung of the Kalahari Desert, whose women will kill a baby born while an older child is still too young to walk. Infanticide was also common on Polynesian islands like Tikopia, where food supplies and population were kept in balance by smothering unwanted newborn infants. In Japan before westernisation, 'mabiki'—a word that has its origins in the thinning of rice seedlings so that there is room for each plant to flourish, but which came to be applied to infanticide too—was very widely practised, not only by peasants with limited amounts of land, but also by those who were quite well off. Even in nineteenth-century Europe, unwanted infants were given to foundling homes run by women known as 'angel makers' because of the very high death rates that occurred.

The fact that infanticide was—and in many parts of the world, still is—widely practised does not, of course, mean that it is right. No argument from 'everyone does this' to 'this is right' can be valid. Even if infanticide could be shown to be the natural response of human beings to the birth of infants born in unfavourable circumstances, that would not make it right. Still, it is worth knowing that from a cross-cultural perspective it is *our* tradition, not that of the Kung or the Japanese, that is unusual in its official morality about infanticide. Recognising that fact puts the modern medical practice of infanticide in a broader perspective.

Euthanasia of Disabled Infants Is Not Morally Acceptable

by Richard Fenigsen

About the author: *Richard Fenigsen is a retired cardiologist from Willem-Alexander Hospital in the Netherlands.*

Active euthanasia has been practiced in the Netherlands since 1972, a time probably much too short to expose all the changes euthanasia brings about in society, but long enough to reveal some of the consequences. Indeed, the practice of euthanasia has perceptibly affected the position of the individual in relation to society, society's very nature and purpose, the law, the government, the judicial system, the family, the expectations of older persons and the prospects of newborn infants, the practice of medicine, and the care of persons with disabilities.

It is important to realize that among the industrialized nations Holland has developed one of the best, and arguably the best, health care system and an excellent system of care for older persons and people with disabilities. Practically all residents have health insurance that covers all essential expenses, including the costs of a prolonged or terminal illness. Money matters play no role in a patient's decisions concerning medical treatment. A high percentage of physicians practice family medicine, which makes health care eminently accessible. There are no crowded emergency rooms. Nursing homes and institutions for mentally retarded persons are modern, well equipped, and manned by skilled and dedicated workers.

Now in the country where so much has been and still is being done to secure good and lifelong care for everybody, the lives of many people are deliberately put to an end, and this happens sometimes upon the request of the person in question and sometimes without his or her request, consent, or knowledge. . . .

Excerpted from Richard Fenigsen, "Physician-Assisted Death in the Netherlands: Impact on Long-Term Care." Reprinted by permission of the publisher, *Issues in Law & Medicine*, vol. 11, no. 3, Winter 1995. Copyright © 1995 by the National Legal Center for the Medically Dependent & Disabled, Inc.

Infant Euthanasia for Disabilities

An estimate of euthanasia on newborn babies and infants up to three months after birth was published by the Royal Dutch Society of Medicine in 1988. Annually, three hundred babies disabled due to extreme prematurity, birth trauma, spina bifida, or Down syndrome are starved and dehydrated to death or denied lifesaving surgery; ten babies with disabilities receive lethal injections each year.

A Committee of the Royal Dutch Society of Medicine stated that termination of life of a newborn is justified if the child almost certainly would have an unliveable life. However, the question should be asked, What kind of life is "unliveable," not for the parents, the doctor, or the ethicist, but for the child involved? In practice, the lives of children with Down syndrome are terminated, although it is well known that people with this disability enjoy their lives. These lives clearly are not unliveable but simply unwanted by the parents and unacceptable for others.

There may be disagreements between the persons who decide, but if the doctor and the parents agree on euthanasia, the life of the child will be terminated.

According to the Royal Society's Committee, when the life of a disabled newborn is terminated, this should be done by refraining from lifesaving medical interventions and depriving the child of food and water; only when this is done and the child does not die, a lethal injection is justified. Again, the practice in some cases departs from the official advice, and doctors proceed directly to administering the lethal injections.

Examples of Euthanasia

The individual cases become known when published in professional journals, when somebody opposed to the termination of the child's life calls in help from outside the hospital, or when the perpetrator or the authorities put the case to trial in order to establish a legal precedent.

The justifications and the circumstances of euthanasia on newborns and children are illustrated by the following published case histories:

1. A baby born with Down syndrome vomited all nourishment and was admitted to one of the country's leading centers for pediatric surgery, the Sophia Hospital in Rotterdam. It was found that the child had an inborn defect of the digestive tract, duodenal atresia, which made it impossible for food to pass from the stomach to the intestines. In these cases, surgery to remove the obstruction is feasible and lifesaving. However, the parents and the pediatric surgeon, Professor J.C. Molenaar, decided to refrain from surgery and let the child die. The family physician, who could not reconcile himself with

"The practice of euthanasia has perceptibly affected . . . the care of persons with disabilities."

161

putting the child to death, called the district attorney. The latter warned the Council for Children's Protection, but this body decided not to intervene. No surgery was done and the child died. A court, and then the Supreme Court, exonerated the surgeon. The family physician was harshly criticized because by calling the DA he broke his oath of confidentiality.

The case provoked a broad discussion, which took an unexpected turn: Many debaters condemned Professor Molenaar's course of action. The Minister of Welfare, Health, and Culture declared that medical treatment should never be refused on the grounds of mental handicap. There was no doubt that the case was just one example of a more widespread practice. Indeed, a team of anesthetists at a teaching hospital decided never to provide anesthesia for cardiac surgery in children with Down syndrome; and there were reports of three children with this syndrome who were denied vitally important surgery for their inborn cardiac defects. The parents persevered and finally found hospitals that accepted the children for surgery.

> *"In practice, the lives of children with Down syndrome are terminated, although it is well known that people with this disability enjoy their lives."*

Refusal to Treat Disabled Children

2. A girl born prematurely, in the thirty-second week, recovered from an infection, but there was a suspicion of intracranial bleeding. This was followed by accumulation of intracranial fluid. The parents refused to allow the insertion of a drainage tube or shunt. On the thirtieth day after birth the child was killed by the pediatrician with injections of a morphine-like drug and potassium chloride.

3. After consulting several specialists and getting the approval of the parents, Dr. Henk Prins, an obstetrician, killed a girl born with spina bifida and hydrocephalus. . . .

4. Danny had spina bifida and hydrocephalus but was in fair general condition. No drainage tube to relieve the hydrocephalus was inserted. Once Danny seemed to have some abdominal pain, and another time he apparently felt not quite well for two consecutive days. This prompted the parents to ask for euthanasia. With this purpose the child was admitted to Rainier de Graaf Hospital in Delft. One of the nurses opposed the decision, and on the next day she and her husband offered to adopt the child. The offer was rejected. On August 19, 1990, Danny, then aged three and one-half months, was killed with drugs administered by intravenous drip. The nurse was reprimanded because by involving her husband in the adoption offer she violated professional confidentiality. . . .

The following case, published in the *Dutch Medical Journal*, is a very different story.

5. This six-year-old boy's intelligence seemed below average. His upbringing presented some problems. He lived with his parents and attended a school for

children requiring special care. Then juvenile diabetes mellitus was discovered. Patients with this type of diabetes must receive injections of insulin; otherwise they develop severe disturbances in metabolism (ketoacidosis), become comatose, and die. The family physician did not ask the parents for permission to start the insulin treatment. Instead, he asked them whether their son should be treated. The parents chose not to treat the child, and the boy died.

The Effect of Euthanasia on Long-Term Care

The problem has not been studied in a systematic way. What we know is based on observations and statements of the caregivers and the recorded experiences of the parents. I focus on the care for mentally disabled persons because more is known about this group than about any other.

Professor J. Stolk of the Free University in Amsterdam, an authority on mental retardation, expressed in 1988 the opinion that "the killing of handicapped children . . . denotes the end, or in any case the beginning of the end of care for the mentally retarded."

Let me summarize Professor Stolk's analysis and the observations of his collaborators that led him to such a conclusion. The care for mentally retarded persons is, and must be, a responsibility shared by the parents with the community. On the basis of such cooperation the care for mentally disabled persons developed and flourished in the Netherlands in the 1960s and 1970s. Institutions shelter about thirty thousand residents, and various intermediate forms of care have been created: small "family-substituting"

> *"A team of anesthetists at a teaching hospital decided never to provide anesthesia for cardiac surgery in children with Down syndrome."*

homes for thirteen thousand working inmates, day care facilities for those living with their families, and "phasing-out" homes. Due to the intermediate forms of care a partly sheltered integration into society of many mentally disabled persons became possible. The contribution of parents was important and necessary for the success of these endeavors. "It seemed that if there were limits to the extension of care, they only could be due to the limited funding, never to lack of commitment."

However, in the last years the commitment of society could no longer be taken for granted. The limits of care have become visible, and parents are often thrown upon their own resources.

Expressions of Hatred Toward Children with Disabilities

But the parents who undertake to raise a disabled child, and those who have for years nursed, loved, and protected their disabled son or daughter, can no more expect support or even understanding of other members of the community. What they now hear are utterances expressing surprise, incomprehension, repugnance, or even hate, warnings, and threats. The following are the examples collected by Stolk: "What? Is that child still alive?" "How can one love such a child?" "Nowadays such a being need not be born at all." "With such a child you put your own future at risk." "Such a thing should have been given an injection."

How do the parents react? As they told the researcher, after such encounters they were left "speechless," "crying and sleepless for several days and nights," "paralyzed," or "totally crushed." A father said: "We feel that people let us down."

Thus both components of the excellent Dutch long-term care of people who are mentally disabled are now strained. Restrictions are felt in the institutional sector, while the families caring for their disabled children are being discouraged. Moreover, long-term care may come to an abrupt end when a medical intervention is needed.

6. Sandra, a spastic and mentally disabled girl of eight, developed a menacing growth on her neck. The mother brought her to a hospital, but the doctor said: "I won't do anything. It's meaningless, anyway." "We fled from that hospital," says the mother.

The caregivers were alarmed by the new regulations concerning euthanasia, proposed by the government in 1991. The regulations acknowledge the existence of euthanasia without request of the patient and do not explicitly preclude euthanasia on persons who are mentally disabled. The president of the Dutch Association for Care of the Disabled, Mr. Bottelier, demanded from the government an assurance that the lives of children who are mentally disabled would be respected. Responding to such demands and to parliamentary questioning, the Minister of Justice and a deputy representing the governing coalition explained that inquiries will be launched in cases of termination of life without the patient's request, and that the lives of incompetent persons will be better protected by a requirement to report euthanasia of these patients than without such a legal requirement. However, it was pointed out by an expert that doctors who wish to avoid inquiry simply do not report such cases.

"Whoever supports the killing of severely disabled newborns, or defends such practice," says Professor Stolk, "takes every argument away from those who try to protect . . . the handicapped in later life."

Disabled Persons Have the Right to Assisted Suicide

by Arnold R. Beisser

About the author: *Arnold R. Beisser is a professor of psychiatry at the University of California at Los Angeles. He is the author of* A Graceful Passage: Notes on the Freedom to Live or Die, *from which the following viewpoint is taken.*

The urgency of dealing with my own life was greatly heightened by a startling hallucination that awakened me one morning—a stentorian voice prophesying that I would die in 1,500 days.

Although a disturbing experience, the event served a useful purpose. It focused my attention on the fact that I'd better start living the way I wanted and at each moment.

Making Changes

Ever since I had become disabled, I had been trying to prove to myself and the world that I was as good as other people, and could do almost anything they could do. Very often I would act as if I did not need help when I did, and so was in considerable pain and discomfort. The only person I had been fooling, though, was myself.

I also did too many things out of fear and insecurity. I had been unnecessarily cautious in a lot of ways, staying in jobs longer than necessary, doing things I no longer wanted to do or believed in.

I was the director of an educational and research center for social and community psychiatry that I had started several years before. It was a great place to work, giving me interesting colleagues, important work, security and a good salary. And I could do my own teaching and research.

There was just one problem: In spite of all of the advantages, my heart was no longer in it. I was just hanging on for all the wrong reasons: I thought it made me look good, it gave me some petty power over others, and it gave me a feeling of security.

When I was brutally frank with myself, I could see another important reason for making a change. It was something that should have been obvious, but that I did not want to admit. My health had declined, and I was no longer up to the physical demands of doing the job well. As soon as I was able to extricate myself, with many regrets, I left.

With the energy I had remaining, I began doing only things I wanted to do, things that I felt competent to do, and things that I placed value on. Seeing patients, teaching and writing were among them. When I was doing them, I felt "all there," not only half there as I had felt sometimes before.

Now I was fully absorbed in what I did, so absorbed that I stopped watching the calendar. I did not realize it when my 1,500 days had passed.

That is the way I hoped I could lead the rest of my life: so completely involved in things I valued that I would not notice when the day I was supposed to die came and went. This is what is meant by a good death, living a full life until the end.

God's or Man's Will?

Jesus and Socrates are dominant figures in the spiritual and intellectual life of Western civilization. Each was persecuted, tried and killed for his beliefs and commitments. Yet, in spite of the judgments, for two millenniums their lives and ideas have served as inspiration and guidance for those seeking a better world.

Jesus was only about 33 at the time of his death. He held beliefs that were alien to his people and criminal in the eyes of their conquerors. His most loyal supporters left him at the time of his greatest need. And, because he declared himself the son of God, his tormentors placed a crown of thorns upon his head. On the cross he was hung by nails driven through his flesh, and left to suffer until death mercifully freed him.

Socrates, the great Athenian philosopher, died at age 70, surrounded by his friends and disciples. He had been charged with the "corruption of the young" and "neglect of the gods" when some of his former students began to challenge the existing order. The only defense he was willing to offer was further avowal of his teaching. He was sentenced to death, and died quickly after drinking the poisonous hemlock.

> *"This is what is meant by a good death, living a full life until the end."*

Although Socrates had a good death and Jesus suffered a terrible one, both accepted their fates willingly, because the alternative was to give up what gave meaning to their lives.

Some would like to reduce the question of life or death to a choice between God's will or man's will. But how can we be certain of what God's will is? We have already interfered with nature in so many ways, that what is natural—what is "God's will"—is very difficult to discern.

Deciding to Live

When I was first sick and hovered between life and death, I was surrounded by loved ones. Family and friends served a constant vigil. I got hundreds of letters and calls. It would have been a good death in many respects.

Then, much of the support began to fade. After all, how long can people maintain hope and continue to disrupt their own lives?

I wanted to be dead, but I could find no way of taking my life since I could not move. I had no choice; I had to live, and it became a good life. The important thing is that it came to have meaning for me, and as long as it does, I hope to live.

> *"The universal threat is the extended, painful, meaningless life—not the death of the body."*

Because I am now 63 and death is no longer so remote, many of my contemporaries and I often speak of it. Although there are differences in how they plan to handle the situation, their fears remain the same. The universal threat is the extended, painful, meaningless life—not the death of the body.

Soon there will come a time when I will no longer be able to be or do what has useful meaning for me. I, too, hope I will not have to linger very long then.

No one who wants his life to continue and can find meaning in it should ever have it taken from him. But for those whose physical, mental and spiritual resources have been spent, and who see no purpose in continuing in agony, we need a way to release them with dignity and support in accordance with their wishes. We must seek new ways to express the faith and compassion of Jesus with the rationality and reason of Socrates.

A Petition for Assisted Suicide

In California a few years ago, a woman named Elizabeth Bouvia petitioned the court to allow her to die. She was born with cerebral palsy, making speech and movement nearly impossible. Through years of arduous effort, she learned to speak, although not clearly. A wheelchair allowed her to move about.

She displayed great courage in trying to lead a "normal" life. She received a master's degree and became a social worker. She later married and kept house. In spite of her severe disabilities, she had done everything within her power to overcome them.

After a time, she developed a painfully incapacitating arthritis. Her marriage failed, and she was no longer employable. She was in continuous pain and lay bedridden in a hospital. Then all pain medication was withheld because of fear that she was becoming addicted.

She was alone and without substantial hope of improvement. Because she was unable to move from her bed, there was no way she could take her own life. So she petitioned the court to help her die.

The media reactions were, in essence, "How dare she affront society by this request?" Bouvia's very personal plight was lost in the ideological polemics that ensued.

I do not question the sincerity of those who spoke out, nor do I doubt that their causes have merit. But the real tragedy is that the fate of this one human being was completely out of her hands, and had become a matter for public policy debate.

Those who ignore the person in favor of the cause must never have experienced, or conveniently have forgotten, what pain, incapacity and hospitalization are like. So they doubt the sincerity of someone like Bouvia.

What they cannot imagine is the eroding effect of the continuous struggle, without respite. The will is slowly drained until nothing remains, and the only hope is in the peace of death.

Although no one can ever completely deny recovery as a possibility, Bouvia could not reasonably expect improvement. Moreover, she was young and could expect to live for many more hopeless years.

Perhaps some people, in similar circumstances, could find some meaning in life. But the important point is that Bouvia could not, and it was she who had to face each day. . . .

Differences in the Quality of Life

We cannot allow ourselves to become so enamored with our scientific and technological advances that we forget what is more basic. We are in danger of being able to sustain biological life while we forget why.

Consider the case of a person who is paralyzed and cannot speak, and who requires nursing help around the clock. The condition is progressive and, inexorably, will lead to death.

If the person is Stephen Hawking, one of the world's most distinguished mathematicians, then he is very much alive and at the pinnacle of his career. Now in his 40s, he is so alive that, to promote his best-selling book, he engaged in a strenuous travel and speaking schedule (his lectures delivered via speech synthesizer).

"The real tragedy is that the fate of this one human being was completely out of her hands."

His life has meaning and significance to others and to himself. Though his condition is progressive, it is very slowly so, and he is not in pain. His mind is not only unimpaired, but he also is a great inspiration to all. He does not want to die, and he has work to do.

But what if he is a different person, in his 80s? He, like Hawking, cannot care for himself; but, unlike the mathematician, is indifferently cared for in a nursing home and his family and friends are gone. He has continuous pain and has become addicted to medications. He moans in pain whenever he is touched or moved. Each time a doctor visits, the man pleads, "Please make me die."

Who is Really Alive?

Is he alive, or only the shell that once contained the man? Is there meaning in his life, and if so, to whom?

Hawking's body barely remains alive, but his mind and spirit are in full flower. The other man's body barely lives, and the main evidences of mind and spirit come from his cries of pain.

So the differences between life and death are such arbitrary "calls" that they cannot be reliably used in practical concerns of when to live and when to die. We must look somewhere else to find our way.

Death Can Be Preferable

The fact is that although our society is willing to provide the resources to keep people alive, very often it is unable to change the conditions that for some make death preferable.

Even the most preliminary consideration of honoring someone's wish to die causes me to recoil. To support people in ending their lives is the antithesis of my life's commitment to save lives.

Yet I would consider death as an option for myself. Should I not be willing to do for others what I would want for myself?

Of course there are other good reasons for reluctance: the fear that someone who did not want it, or who might recover, was put to death. It is the one mistake that cannot be repaired.

But if one has the audacity to become a physician, one encounters life-and-death decisions each day. Although most are not clear-cut and have considerable margin for error, both doctors and patients think that making the decision is worth the risk. Is it not also worth the risk when we consider a patient's desire to die?

Assisted Suicide Devalues the Lives of Disabled People

by Joseph P. Shapiro

About the author: *Joseph P. Shapiro is a senior editor for* U.S. News & World Report. *His articles on disability and social policy issues have appeared in numerous publications, including* U.S. News & World Report, *the* Progressive, *the* Disability Rag, *and the* Washington Post.

The intensive care unit was the wrong place to put a young man like Larry James McAfee. It was a stopping-off point for patients near death. But McAfee was not dying; he wasn't even sick. Trapped in his hospital bed, he felt as if the weeks were ticking off in slow motion while around him the intensive care unit seemed to whir at hyperspeed. Patients were wheeled in from surgery or wheeled out to the morgue, nurses and doctors hurried through, machines hummed, and lights glared. After three months, in the spring of 1989, McAfee, fed up, called a lawyer with a request. Help me, he said, "I want to die."

A Plan for Suicide

Larry McAfee, then thirty-four years old, was a quadriplegic, the result of a motorcycle accident in the mountains of northern Georgia. The muscles that worked McAfee's lungs and air sacs were paralyzed from his injury. So a respirator, which was attached by a tube inserted down his throat, pushed air into his lungs to make him breathe. McAfee's request for the right to die brought Fulton County Superior Court Judge Edward Johnson quickly to Atlanta's Grady Memorial Hospital for an unusual bedside court hearing. Life as a quadriplegic, sustained by a machine and dependent on attendants for everything from eating to coughing, had been "intolerable," McAfee told the judge in the ICU. He spoke in a strained voice—unanimated, almost robotic—trying to be heard over the soft whooshing sound of the air passing through his respirator. He recounted how he had been moved from one far-flung nursing home to another and that he no longer foresaw a life out of a hospital bed. "It is very heartbreaking," McAfee said to the judge. "Everyday when I wake up there is nothing to look forward to."

McAfee, an engineering student, even told the judge how he planned to end his life. The method had come to him while he had been lying in the ICU. He described the device he invented to kill himself in the same matter-of-fact tone he would use to explain any other engineering project. It consisted of a time switch, one relay, and two valves. The simple invention would force the air from the respirator to spill ineffectually into the room instead of into his lungs, without setting off the alarm. A friend would assemble it according to McAfee's instructions. Someone else, with permission from the court, would help McAfee swallow a sedative. Then, before he drifted into a deep sleep, McAfee would clench a mouthstick between his teeth and use it to turn on the timer. It would tick off the last seconds of air pumped into his lungs. Death would come—gently, comfortably—in his drug-induced sleep.

> *"Larry McAfee's story was . . . another chilling reminder of how a disabled life was dismissed—by doctors, judges, and the public— as a devalued life."*

Three weeks later, the judge summoned McAfee's parents and three younger sisters to his chambers. Johnson would allow the young quadriplegic to end his life. They all cried, and tears came to the judge's eyes. McAfee's mother hugged the judge and thanked him for his compassion. "That was the hardest decision of my life," he told Amelia McAfee. "But that young man made the biggest impression on me of any young man in my life."

Failing to Help the Disabled

To disabled people, however, Larry McAfee's story was not a simple right-to-die case. Instead, it was another chilling reminder of how a disabled life was dismissed—by doctors, judges, and the public—as a devalued life. As they viewed it, a judge saw a man with a translucent plastic coil connecting a hole in his throat to a machine and eagerly ruled this a life not worth living. It did not matter that about fifteen thousand Americans living outside of hospitals use respirators. A nondisabled man who asked the state to help him take his life would get suicide-prevention counseling, but McAfee had not been considered rash or even depressed. Instead, a judge had praised him as sensible and brave. It was a bitter insult to the millions of other people with disabilities who were living successfully on their own—including those so severely disabled that they used respirators daily.

From a disability rights point of view, the McAfee decision was better understood as the story of how this country fails miserably to care for severely disabled people. Instead of getting help to live on his own, McAfee was sentenced to indifferent nursing homes and hospitals and stripped of basic decision making about his life. It is not an ignorant system. Rehabilitation therapists have perfected programs for returning injured people to their homes to live and their jobs for work. There is astounding technology—like the wheelchair McAfee could control with his mouth and the portable respirator that fits on its back—to allow for new levels of independence. Nor is the system a stingy one. Over $1.5 million in private insurance, state Medicaid, federal Medicare, and Social Security payments was spent on McAfee in the four and a half years between his accident and the final court decision.

Misplaced Generosity

But the generosity was often misspent and misplaced. For example, state Medicaid would pay every penny of McAfee's expenses in a nursing home. Yet it would not pay one cent for what he needed to live at home so that he could go back to work and be a taxpayer instead of simply taking welfare. Social Security and Medicaid are based on out-of-date assumptions that severely disabled people simply need support payments to be attended by family or in a nursing home because they are close to death and can expect little more. This may have been true as recently as Medicaid and Medicare's inception in 1965. Indeed, it has been only in recent decades that someone with an injury like McAfee's had even reasonable odds of survival. Kidney infection and bedsores quickly took the

> *"Instead of getting help to live on his own, McAfee was sentenced to indifferent nursing homes and hospitals and stripped of basic decision making about his life."*

lives of those who lived past their initial injury. Today, doctors save eight thousand people a year who become paralyzed by accidents, from nightmarish highway smashups to mundane slips in the bathtub. There are some 250,000 survivors of spinal cord injuries nationwide .

McAfee was victimized not by a mean-spirited system, just a life-deadening one. Many severely disabled people hold jobs, live in their own homes, marry, and bring up families. Many others, like McAfee, get exhausted trying to cope. Clinical psychologist Carol Gill, a quadriplegic who uses a wheelchair and specializes in counseling disabled clients dealing with depression, calls what McAfee went through "disability burnout." She describes it as the frustration of trying to work through an unresponsive and bureaucratic system of health care that too often promises more than it delivers.

Anger and Despair

When I met McAfee I found a man angry about his loss of control over his body but more angry still about his loss of control over his life. He was living in a gloomy Alabama nursing home room, his bed separated by a pink curtain from the next bed, which had been home to a succession of elderly men on respirators. McAfee was a large man—he stood six feet, six inches before the accident—propped on his side in a hospital bed. He had no shirt on, and his body was covered by a white blanket. Nurses had not bothered to shave him, and there was a three-day-old stubble on his face. Out the window next to his bed, he could see only sky and desolate trees. A stack of unopened mail sat on the windowsill, along with a bouquet of balloons from his mother and a framed picture of an attractive woman in a nurse's uniform. McAfee spoke in a distant, distracted voice,

> *"Clinical psychologist Carol Gill . . . calls what McAfee went through 'disability burnout.'"*

except when describing the pain of his lowly status as a disabled man. "You're looked upon as a second-rate citizen," he said, the bitterness rising in his voice. "People say, 'You're using my taxes. You don't deserve to be here. You should hurry up and leave.'" Nurses and doctors talked about his prognosis and problems while standing at the bottom of his bed, as if he were invisible. Attendants pulled his body roughly, at times dropping him to the floor, and some, he felt, made it clear they considered caring for him a loathsome chore. "I didn't ask to be like this at all," McAfee said. "You reach a point where you just can't take it anymore."

At the time of his accident, the man his family called "Bubba" was close to completing his engineering degree at Georgia Tech in Atlanta, while he worked full-time at an engineering firm. He was bright and had an aptitude for math, but he never applied himself in school, either at the private academy in rural Sandersville where he finished high school or in college. He planned to become a mechanical engineer. He had a girlfriend in Atlanta but was not ready for marriage. After the accident, in his self-pity, he ended their relationship, even though she had remained supportive.

It is a myth that being disabled means being in bad health. A person may need a wheelchair for help in moving or a respirator for help in breathing yet live a long and healthy life. McAfee's health was in danger for the two weeks after the accident. At Georgia Baptist Hospital, McAfee was stabilized. Holes were drilled into his skull to attach a brace for traction. Another hole was opened in his throat to insert the plastic tube from the respirator. Once his health improved, he was sent to Atlanta's Shepherd Spinal Center. Quadriplegia means full or partial paralysis of the arms and legs. In rare cases, quadriplegics, like James Shepherd, who founded the Atlanta center after being injured in 1973 while body surfing on a beach in Rio de Janeiro, Brazil, can even walk with the aid of crutches. "High quads" like McAfee, who have had injuries to the top vertebrae in their spinal column, are completely paralyzed below the neck. Their internal organs—kidneys and liver, for example—still work. . . .

Chapter 4

A Right to Die?

Legal doctrine firmly supports a person's right to refuse medical treatment. . . . To let McAfee turn off his respirator, the judge concluded, would merely be allowing the "injury process to take its natural course." In other words, McAfee would not be committing suicide. He would be dying from the injury of the motorcycle accident of more than four years before. Johnson never considered how the health care system had failed McAfee and even contributed to his wanting to end his life. Instead, Johnson spoke of the tragedy of the "boy who loved sports" and "teased his sisters" before the accident but who, as a disabled man, could no longer find "quality in his existence."

Disability activists in Atlanta reacted with a visceral anger. It was as if McAfee's decision to die—and the sympathetic nods of approval from both church and state—were a direct judgment that their lives were not worth living either. Mark Johnson and Eleanor Smith, two Atlanta-based activists, led demonstrations outside the courtroom. If McAfee could end his life, they asked, didn't that mean the state put a lower value on the life of a disabled person than on the life of a nondisabled one? Why should there be an exception to the ban on state-assisted suicide only because a man was disabled? The activists feared that the court ruling sent a message that disabled people had a duty to die rather than be a burden to their families and society. Because of McAfee's paralysis, the judge's ruling was considered a humane gesture. Yet had McAfee gone to court but not been disabled, a team of psychiatrists would have been dispatched to lift him from his depression and give him suicide-prevention counseling, argued Smith. . . .

Devalued Lives

To the disability activists, McAfee's case was an example of a disabled life devalued. It was a reminder of the many other cases where an easy right to die was extended to a disabled person as an act of compassion. In 1983, Elizabeth Bouvia, a twenty-six-year-old social worker with severe cerebral palsy, checked into a Los Angeles hospital and asked for painkillers while she starved herself to death. With the help of an American Civil Liberties Union attorney, she argued that her severe disability made her want to die and that she had a right to refuse life-saving treatment. Three mental health professionals who examined her agreed but ignored the recent emotional crises in her life. She had lost a child to miscarriage and her marriage had broken up; her brother had died; she was financially troubled and had been forced to withdraw from graduate school. A California judge also ignored her depression and concluded that the hospital should help Bouvia die, given "her helpless and, to her,

> *"Attendants pulled [McAfee's] body roughly, at times dropping him to the floor."*

174

intolerable condition." But Bouvia was far from being the helpless woman described by the judge. Instead, as historian Paul Longmore noted, she "is a woman who operated a power wheelchair, was halfway toward a master's degree, married, made love with her husband and planned to become a mother. This is a woman who still could and might do all of those things if she were given appropriate psychiatric and medical treatment."

> *"Activists feared that the court ruling sent a message that disabled people had a duty to die rather than be a burden to their families and society."*

Bouvia set the case law that a patient could refuse treatment, regardless of his or her motives, age, or health. Her struggle got nationwide press attention. Less well remembered is that Bouvia never followed through on her death wish. Nor did she get the support she needed to live independently. A reporter in 1988 found Bouvia in a Los Angeles hospital, living in a tiny, $800-a-day isolation room and registered as "Jane Doe," still talking of wanting to die. . . .

A Rescue Attempt

By the time Johnson made his ruling, McAfee was in a new nursing home in Alabama. That complicated McAfee's ability to end his life, since the court order applied only to Georgia. . . .

There was pressure for McAfee to end his life quickly. The state attorney general had asked the Georgia Supreme Court to set guidelines for future McAfee cases. It was possible that the higher court would overturn Judge Johnson's decision. Despite saying he still wanted to die, McAfee took no steps to be returned to Georgia. In 1989, a few days before Thanksgiving, the state supreme court upheld McAfee's right to end his life. But McAfee's slowness to act seemed to prove right his opponents. They had argued that his legal suit did not reflect a sincere death wish but an angry lashing out at the way the health care system had mistreated him. This ambivalence gave a group of people an opportunity to befriend McAfee in an eleventh-hour attempt to save his life.

Pivotal in this effort was Russ Fine, who latched on to McAfee as his defender and, no matter how sullen McAfee's moods, never let go. Fine was not a disability rights activist, although he was the director of the injury prevention research center at the University of Alabama, studying ways to prevent the kind of accidents that had made McAfee a quadriplegic. Preventable injuries, including vehicular accidents, falls, drownings, and fires, are the biggest cause of death and disablement, notes Fine. However, the most militant disability activists are wary of injury prevention specialists like Fine, since, they argue, to prevent disability is to suggest there is something pejorative about it. "We want more disabled people, not fewer," was the sardonic explanation of the late Timothy Cook, director of the National Disability Law Center, whose point was that prevention is a health issue, not a disability issue. Fine got through to McAfee in part because he did not bring a strong ideology with him. He simply wanted to show McAfee that there could be a better life. Fine made it clear from the beginning that he supported McAfee's right to end his life. But he wanted the disabled man to pursue all his options first. McAfee was openly skeptical and gave Fine little sign of encouragement. He had heard all the promises of independence before—starting at Shepherd—but found they were hollow if the only option was to live in a nursing home or a hospital ICU.

"Larry McAfee is the embodiment of everything that is wrong with the health care delivery and reimbursement system today. It is high tech and low touch," said Fine. "By that I mean we have the technology literally to resurrect the near-dead but not the additional components to address quality of life. The question becomes, Whose needs are we addressing? Are we doing it for our colleagues and professional peers just so we can go to meetings and deliver papers? Do we just want to demonstrate our prowess and expertise in maintaining life in catastrophic illness injuries, where a generation ago our predecessors couldn't do it?"

> "We have the technology literally to resurrect the near-dead but not the additional components to address quality of life."

It was Fine's unconventional manner that eventually led McAfee to trust him. Despite being a health care professional himself, Fine shared McAfee's sneering impatience for the officious nursing home staffers who were constantly citing their rules and demanding that McAfee, like some naughty schoolboy, obey them or be sent back to Grady Hospital. Over the objections of the nursing home staff, Fine brought McAfee the beers and copies of *Playboy* he had been denied. He set up a VCR in McAfee's room and brought an occasional soft-porn movie, and then raised hell when the offended nurses unplugged McAfee's television. "The guy is still a young male," said Fine. "That gets to the quality-of-life issue. They're deciding what he sees. What kind of crap is that?"

Technological Independence

Others worked to show McAfee that he could live independently. Engineer Rick Rice hooked up an environmental control system, a remote-control device that McAfee could activate with his voice in order to work the telephone and television in his nursing home room. Kirk Tcherneshoff, a paraplegic who ran the local independent living center, took him in his van on a shopping outing. Gary Edwards, the director of United Cerebral Palsy of Birmingham—who saw McAfee, like his own clients, fighting an indifferent bureaucracy to live independently—added his own vast understanding of how to wade through the social welfare funding system. His assistant, Brenda Carson, figured out ways a quadriplegic could work as an engineer. . . .

176

The Turning Point

With his parents and the group of activists fighting hard to change his mind, McAfee began to waver. Particularly crucial was another machine—a voice-activated computer that cost five thousand dollars. With it, McAfee could put to work his training as an engineer. Bob Stockwell, a California computer specialist, saw a television news report on McAfee and flew to Alabama to set up the computer for him. The computer was programmed to recognize the sound of his voice. McAfee could turn it on and off and command it to do many tasks just by speaking. With special software, he could make sharp architectural renderings of

> *"Medicaid and Medicare policies that do not work in the best interest of the disabled have caused me and those like me to become prisoners of bureaucracy."*

buildings and apartment layouts by drawing on the computer screen with a sonar beam directed from a band strapped to his head. He drew by moving his head, and the beam went with it. But when the computer first arrived at the nursing home, nurses would not let McAfee set it up, saying that the institution could not be "liable" for the expensive equipment in case it was stolen. Fine got McAfee's doctor to overrule the nurses and soon McAfee was practicing a few hours a day to the point that he was good enough to show off his skills to a prospective employer.

The computer excited McAfee. For the first time he talked of preferring to live, instead of dying. By February 21, 1990, when he was invited to speak before the Georgia State Senate, McAfee sounded like a full-blown disability rights activist. "Medicaid and Medicare policies that do not work in the best interest of the disabled have caused me and those like me to become prisoners of bureaucracy," said McAfee, from his wheelchair on the floor of the senate, as Fine held a microphone to his mouth. He had been turned into a "prisoner of fate and bad luck," he said, by "a bureaucracy that will pay for the warehousing of the disabled but one that does not address or even consider the quality of our shattered lives.". . .

A New Life of Hope

On July 11, 1990, McAfee, in his puff-and-sip wheelchair, boarded an ambulance van and was driven to Augusta, Georgia. Medicaid officials had insisted that he stay at the Medical College of Georgia Hospital for evaluation. But after a month he was moved to a new group home in Augusta. . . . There was a round-the-clock attendant, accessible bathrooms and kitchen. There was space for McAfee's computer. Within a year, a few other severely disabled Georgians moved in. Johnson said he hoped the facility would be a model for the nation. Later, Georgia started a new program to give severely disabled people money for attendant care, one that would give recipients broad control that is rare in choosing and hiring attendants. It took over a year, however, for Georgia Medicaid to buy the additional computer equipment that it promised to purchase McAfee and that delayed their helping him find work. But McAfee was freer to get in and out of the house. He took a van to go shopping. He saw his family. His mood bounced up and down, often paralleling occasional respiratory problems. But on the whole, he pronounced himself happy to be alive, living a "good" life that had given him "hope."

Bibliography

Books

Willie V. Bryan   *In Search of Freedom: How Persons with Disabilities Have Been Disenfranchised from the Mainstream of American Society.* Springfield, IL: C.C. Thomas, 1996.

Leah Hager Cohen   *Train Go Sorry: Inside a Deaf World.* New York: Houghton Mifflin, 1994.

Lew Golan   *Reading Between the Lips: A Totally Deaf Man Makes It in the Mainstream.* Chicago: Bonus Books, 1995.

Linda J. Hayes et al., eds.   *Ethical Issues in Developmental Disabilities.* Reno, NV: Context Press, 1994.

John Hockenberry   *Moving Violations: War Zones, Wheelchairs, and Declarations of Independence.* New York: Hyperion, 1995.

Philip K. Howard   *The Death of Common Sense: How Law Is Suffocating America.* New York: Random House, 1994.

Mary Johnson, ed.   *People with Disabilities Explain It All for You.* Louisville, KY: Advocado Press, 1992.

Harlan Lane   *The Mask of Benevolence: Disabling the Deaf Community.* New York: Knopf, 1992.

Jenny Morris   *Pride Against Prejudice: Transforming Attitudes to Disability.* Philadelphia: New Society, 1991.

Oliver W. Sacks   *An Anthropologist on Mars: Seven Paradoxical Tales.* New York: Knopf, 1995.

Lonny Shavelson   *A Chosen Death: The Dying Confront Assisted Suicide.* New York: Simon & Schuster, 1995.

Barrett Shaw, ed.   *The Ragged Edge: The Disability Experience from the Pages of the First Fifteen Years of the* Disability Rag. Louisville, KY: Advocado Press, 1994.

Joni Eareckson Tada   *When Is It Right to Die? Suicide, Euthanasia, Suffering, Mercy.* Grand Rapids, MI: Zondervan, 1992.

Jane West, ed.   *Implementing the Americans with Disabilities Act.* Cambridge, MA: Blackwell, 1996.

Periodicals

Stuart Anderson   "Why Schools Don't Dare to Discipline the Disabled," *Weekly Standard*, February 19, 1996.

Bibliography

Lisa Belkin	"The High Cost of Living," *New York Times Magazine*, January 31, 1993.
Richard V. Burkhauser	"Beyond Stereotypes: Public Policy and the Doubly Disabled," *American Enterprise*, September/October 1992.
J. Byzek	"Stephen and Lydia and Daniel Just Want to Go to School," *Mouth*, July 1995.
Robert F. Drinan	"Are Profoundly Handicapped Children in Catholic Schools Entitled to Government Assistance?" *America*, January 30, 1993.
Thomas E. Elkins	"Ethical Concerns and Future Directions in Maternal Screening for Down Syndrome," *Women's Health Issues*, Spring 1995. Available from Jacobs Institute of Women's Health, 409 Twelfth St. SW, Washington, DC 20024.
Mike Ervin	"Closing the Door on Home Care," *Progressive*, March 1996.
Mike Ervin	"Who Gets to Live? Who Will Decide?" *Progressive*, October 1994.
Chester E. Finn Jr.	"Corrupted Intentions," *National Review*, March 11, 1996.
David Frum	"Oh My Aching . . . You Name It," *Forbes*, April 26, 1993.
Lew Golan	"A Dialogue of the Deaf," *Washington Post National Weekly Edition*, March 25–31, 1996.
Jean Guarino	"Opening Church Doors to People with Disabilities," *St. Anthony Messenger*, June 1996.
Laura Hershey	"Choosing Disability," *Ms.*, July/August 1994.
Leslie Kaufman-Rosen	"Who Are the Disabled?" *Newsweek*, November 7, 1994.
John Leo	"Mainstreaming's 'Jimmy Problem,'" *U.S. News & World Report*, June 27, 1994.
Ricki Lewis	"Choosing a Perfect Child," *World & I*, March 1993. Available from 3600 New York Ave. NE, Washington, DC 20002.
Deborah Lutterbeck	"Government by Tantrum," *Common Cause Magazine*, Summer 1995.
New Internationalist	Special section on the disabled, July 1992.
Fred Pelka	"Attack of the Morally Challenged," *On the Issues*, Summer 1996.
Linda Ransom	"Lawyers May Kill My Daughter," *Wall Street Journal*, March 20, 1996.
John Rennie	"Who Is Normal?" *Scientific American*, August 1993.
Llewellyn H. Rockwell Jr.	"Disabilities Act Goes Too Far and Stifles a Free Economy," *Insight*, September 7, 1992. Available from 3600 New York Ave. NE, Washington, DC 20002.
Llewellyn H. Rockwell Jr.	"Wheelchairs at Third Base," *National Review*, June 7, 1993.
Patti Shanaberg	"Know Your Audience," *Ability*, vol. 95, no. 10, 1996. Available from 1682 Langley Ave., Irvine, CA 92714-56330.
Albert Shanker	"Where We Stand on the Rush to Inclusion," *Vital Speeches of the Day*, March 1, 1994.
B. Shaw	"The 'Race' to Inclusion," *Disability Rag*, May 1994.

The Disabled

Jill Smolowe — "Noble Aims, Mixed Results," *Time*, July 31, 1995.

Sharon White Taylor — "You're in My Spot," *Newsweek*, February 19, 1996.

David Van Biema — "Beyond the Sound Barrier," *Time*, October 3, 1994.

Barbara Vobejda — "The Disabled Fear Losing Financial and Moral Support," *Washington Post National Weekly Edition*, August 14–20, 1995.

David Wasserman — "Disability, Discrimination, and Fairness," *Report from the Institute for Philosophy & Public Policy,* Winter/Spring 1993. Available from the University of Maryland School of Public Affairs, 3rd Fl., College Park, MD 20742.

Kathi Wolfe — "Bashing the Disabled," *Progressive*, November 1995.

Richard Wolkomir — "American Sign Language: 'It's Not Mouth Stuff—It's Brain Stuff,'" *Smithsonian*, July 1992.

Organizations to Contact

The editors have compiled the following list of organizations concerned with the issues debated in this book. The descriptions are derived from materials provided by the organizations themselves. All have publications or information available for interested readers. The list was compiled on the date of publication of the present volume; names, addresses, phone and fax numbers, and e-mail/internet addresses may change. Be aware that many organizations take several weeks or longer to respond to inquiries, so allow as much time as possible.

American Foundation for the Blind (AFB)
11 Penn Plaza, Suite 300
New York, NY 10001
(212) 502-7661
fax: (212) 502-7662

The AFB strives to enable people who are blind or visually impaired to achieve equality of access and opportunity. The foundation educates the public and policymakers about the needs and capabilities of people who are blind or visually impaired. Its numerous publications include the semiannual newsletter *AFB News* and the position paper "The Reauthorization of the Individuals with Disabilities Act: A Reference Guide for Persons Concerned with the Educational Rights of Children Who Are Blind or Visually Impaired."

The Arc
500 E. Boulder St., S-300
Arlington, TX 76010
(817) 261-6003
fax: (817) 277-3491

The Arc helps people with mental retardation to gain autonomy and to realize their goals. It works to reduce the incidence and limit the consequence of mental retardation through education, research, and advocacy. The organization publishes various newsletters, including *The Arc Now*, monthly, and *The Arc Today*, quarterly.

BC Coalition of People with Disabilities (BCCPD)
#204-456 W. Broadway
Vancouver, BC V5Y 1R3
CANADA
(604) 875-0188
fax: (604) 875-9227

BCCPD is an organization run by and for people with disabilities throughout British Columbia. Through its work, the coalition promotes the full participation of people with disabilities in all aspects of society. Among its publications are the newsletter *Transition*, which is published eight times a year, the position paper "A Proposal for a New Definition of 'Handicapped,'" and the pamphlet *Housing for People with Disabilities*.

Cato Institute
1000 Massachusetts Ave., NW
Washington, DC 20001
(202) 842-0200
fax: (202) 842-3490

The Cato Institute is a nonpartisan public policy research foundation dedicated to promoting limited government and individual liberty. The institute believes the Americans with Disabilities Act is not effective and imposes unreasonable costs on businesses. It publishes the quarterly magazine *Regulation* as well as numerous position papers, including "Handicapping Freedom: The Americans with Disabilities Act" and "The Americans with Disabilities Act: Time for Amendments."

Center on Human Policy
School of Education
Syracuse University
805 S. Crouse Ave.
Syracuse, NY 13244-2280
(315) 443-3851
fax: (315) 443-4338
e-mail: thechp@sued.syr.edu

The center works to promote the full inclusion of people with developmental disabilities in community life. It provides information to families, human services professionals, and others on laws, regulations, and programs affecting children and adults with disabilities. Among the center's publications are the books *Christmas in Purgatory: A Photographic Essay on Mental Retardation* and *Ordinary Moments: The Disabled Experience*.

Disabled Peoples' International (DPI)
101-7 Evergreen
Winnipeg, MB R3L 2T3
CANADA
(204) 287-8010
fax: (204) 453-1367
e-mail: dpi@dpi.org

DPI is a development organization established to help disabled people take charge of their lives. It works to achieve equality for disabled people worldwide. Among its numerous publications are the quarterly *Disability International*, the paper "The Role of Disabled Persons' Organizations," and the book *The Last Civil Rights Movement*.

Gazette International Networking Institute (GINI)
4207 Lindell Blvd., #110
St. Louis, MO 63108-2915
(314) 534-0475
fax: (314) 534-5070

GINI is a networking organization that advocates for people with disabilities, particularly polio survivors and users of ventilators. GINI publishes the quarterly *Polio Network News* and the biannual *IVUN News*, which addresses the concerns of ventilator users.

Learning Disabilities Association of America (LDA)
4156 Library Rd.
Pittsburgh, PA 15234-1349
(412) 341-1515
fax: (412) 344-0224

LDA is a national volunteer organization comprising individuals with learning disabilities, their families, and concerned professionals. It works to alleviate the detrimental effects of learning disabilities and supports research on the causes of learning disabilities. LDA publishes the bimonthly newsletter *LDA Newsbriefs* and the semiannual *Learning Disabilities*.

Mainstream
3 Bethesda Metro Center, Suite 830
Bethesda, MD 20814
(301) 654-2400
fax: (301) 654-2403

Mainstream is dedicated to increasing employment opportunities for persons with disabilities. It assists companies and organizations in employing people with disabilities, and it operates the Mainstream Disability Employment Network, which makes referrals to placement services around the country. Mainstream publishes the bimonthly journal *Employment in the Mainstream.*

National Center for Learning Disabilities (NCLD)
381 Park Ave. South, Suite 1420
New York, NY 10016
(212) 545-7510
fax: (212) 545-9665

NCLD promotes public awareness and understanding of children and adults with learning disabilities so that they may achieve their potential and enjoy full participation in society. NCLD publishes the magazine *Their World* once a year and the newsletter *NCLD News* three times a year.

National Center for Youth with Disabilities (NCYD)
University of Minnesota
420 Delaware St. SE
Minneapolis, MN 55455-0392
(612) 626-2825
fax: (612) 626-2134
e-mail: ncyd@gold.tc.umn.edu

NCYD is an information, policy, and resource center that helps adolescents and young adults with chronic illnesses or developmental disabilities to participate in community life and to achieve their goals. It publishes the triannual newsletter *Connections* and the report "Teenagers at Risk: A National Perspective of State Level Services for Adolescents with Chronic Illness or Disability."

National Council on Independent Living (NCIL)
2111 Wilson Blvd., Suite 405
Arlington, VA 22201
(703) 525-3406
fax: (703) 525-3409
e-mail: ncil@tsbbs02.tnet.com
NCIL is the national membership association of local nonprofit corporations known as Independent Living Centers (ILCs). NCIL promotes the full integration and participation of persons with disabilities in society, as well as the development, improvement, and expansion of ILCs. It publishes the quarterly *NCIL Newsletter* and various position papers.

National Down Syndrome Congress (NDSC)
1605 Chantilly Dr., Suite 250
Atlanta, GA 30324-3269
(404) 633-1555
fax: (404) 633-2817

NDSC is a national advocacy organization composed of parents and professionals concerned with Down syndrome. It promotes the belief that persons with Down syndrome have the right to a normal and dignified life, particularly in the areas of education, medical care, employment, and human services. NDSC maintains a comprehensive clearinghouse that provides information and referral services on all aspects of Down syndrome. Among its publications are the *Down Syndrome News*, which is published ten times a year, and the position statement "Quality Education for Students with Down Syndrome."

National Federation of the Blind (NFB)
1800 Johnson St.
Baltimore, MD 21230
(410) 659-9314
fax: (410) 685-5653

The NFB's goal is the complete integration of the blind into society on the basis of equality. It monitors all legislation affecting the blind and evaluates present programs for the blind. The NFB publishes the monthly *Braille Monitor* and the quarterly magazine *Future Reflections*.

National Information Center for Children and Youth with Disabilities (NICHCY)
PO Box 1492
Washington, DC 20013-1492
(202) 884-8200
fax: (202) 884-8441
e-mail: nichcy@aed.org

NICHCY is a clearinghouse that provides information on disabilities and related issues. It assists parents, educators, caregivers, advocates, and others in helping children and youth with disabilities to participate as fully as possible in school, at home, and in the community. NICHCY publishes the annual *Disability Fact Sheet* and the periodic newsletter *News Digest*.

Reason Foundation
3415 S. Sepulveda Blvd., Suite 400
Los Angeles, CA 90034
(310) 391-2245
fax: (310) 391-4395

The Reason Foundation is a national public policy research organization that promotes individual freedoms and libertarian principles. It believes that the Americans with Disabilities Act is too expensive to enforce. It publishes the monthly *Privatization Watch* and the magazine *Reason* eleven times a year.

The Roeher Institute
York University
4700 Keele St.
North York, ON M3J 1P3
CANADA
(416) 661-9611
fax: (416) 661-5701
e-mail: mticoll@orion.yorku.ca

This organization is Canada's national institute for the study of public policy affecting persons with disabilities. It works to support the integration of persons with disabilities into society. The institute publishes the quarterly journal *Entourage*.

Voice of the Retarded (VOR)
5005 Newport Dr., Suite 108
Rolling Meadows, IL 60008
(847) 253-6020
fax: (847) 253-6054

VOR keeps public officials, legislators, and the general public informed about issues that affect persons with mental retardation. It supports alternatives in residential living and rehabilitation systems that best suit the individual needs of people with mental retardation. VOR's publications include the position paper "Voice of the Retarded Statement on Deinstitutionalization," the quarterly newsletter *Voice of the Retarded*, and the biweekly *Office Bulletin*.

Index